CSABA BABAK

BEER MEANS BUSINESS

★ ★ ★

ECONOMICS AND MARKETING IN THE UK BREWING INDUSTRY

RETHINK PRESS

First published in Great Britain 2016

by Rethink Press (www.rethinkpress.com)

© Copyright Csaba Babak

Author's photo © Atef Haikal

CONTENTS

INTRODUCTION

There is plenty of literature relevant to beer. There are books about home or industrial brewing, beer ingredients and recipes, the old and new sorts of beer, breweries and their stories, the history of the brewing industry at large and even the economics of certain aspects thereof. However, there is little to be read about the outlook for this industry, in particular outside of the USA.

The description and scarce data of the evolution of the beer market in North America permeate industry analyses, business documents and the news. This information is typically used out of desperation and only generates more questions than answers, simply prolonging the mystery about what is actually happening in the UK and what is yet to happen.

This book will not dwell on brewing, beers, breweries and the history of the industry. Instead, it focuses as far as possible on the pure economic, business and marketing aspects of beer so as to identify the future opportunities and challenges, as well as different scenarios through the analysis of relevant recent events and the current situation in the wider beer supply chain in the UK.

For this purpose, the book does not follow a particular economic or scientific assessment model. Instead, it relies on the author's pragmatism and a schematic supply chain from farmers to consumers while looking into each distinctive phase. In doing so, the book refrains from naming individual companies, brands or products, or using numbers beyond the purpose of illustration.

Beer Means Business is far from complete or definitive, but it provides a good portion of food for thought for anyone wondering how the new waves in the brewing industry can be surfed sustainably.

WHAT'S BREWING?

THE WIDER ECONOMIC CONTEXT

An ever increasing number of incidents suggests that the ways in which we have gone about things are neither working nor sustainable any more. The world of business has faced significant challenges and suffered most from the economic and financial crisis, the aftermath of which is still lingering around.

It is theoretically impossible that the sum of the growth of parts will exceed the growth of the given economy as a whole. In an environment that has been majorly set back and is slowly recovering, the basic economic principle of sustained growth needs to be reinterpreted. This implies a paradigm shift to accept lower growth rates or discovering new ways and spaces available for further growth. Those who do not respond in either way to the new conditions will struggle to maintain momentum.

Companies still following the practices that have guided their growth so far will only be able to please shareholders by improving efficiency in the long-term and cutting non-essential costs in the short term. The former triggers furthering the economics of scale, not through investment but by integrations, e.g. mergers and acquisitions to leverage synergies of operations. The latter, though, immediately affects the people involved. Generosity left along with prosperity. Employees' notions of a career, as well as their sense of security and risks associated with their employment, change in these corrupt systems. Being hired is an indication of their capability to carry out a dedicated task rather than the potential they bring into the company; the performance of employees who take on a specific task improves with experience and specialisation. They are then more likely to be transferred between similar roles within or across companies, otherwise their transition requires training. In addition, human labour is reportedly becoming more and more redundant in developed economies, either due to automation or globalisation making more price-competitive human labour available.

Consequently, the idea of a life-long employment and career gives comfort only to those who still believe that the sacrifices of the present, their patience and exploitation, will be rewarded somewhere in the distant future. The actual outlook of benefiting from retirement is rather more grim.

The difference between the levels of perceived risk in the corporate world and that of self-employment has diminished. The safety of remaining faceless in a corporation and needing to show up for a limited group of people believed to influence their career is less attractive for more and more people in comparison to the real satisfaction of actual creation and authority. This, in combination with the realisation of the need for a paradigm shift in economy, initiated the rise of passionate endeavours that are far more exciting and fulfilling: part-time activities originally set out for self-amusement or potential extra income eventually turn into successful businesses.

The new paradigms have brought fresh ideas, innovation and art into the world of business, as well as more agility and competitiveness in the marketplace. Small businesses, ranging from heart-centred sole traders to capitalist start-ups, have established the models that are alternative to simply capitalising on one's labour and time.

The proliferation of businesses based on the alternative models of more satisfaction and greater potential is, in fact, a new wave – something that has penetrated the beer industry too.

THE C-WORD

Definitions of craft (noun) from the *Oxford Advanced Learner's Dictionary*:

- [countable, uncountable] An activity involving a special skill at making things with your hands

- [singular] All the skills needed for a particular activity

- [uncountable] (formal, disapproving) Skill in making people believe what you want them to believe.

In fact, the dictionary does not have any definition of craft as an adjective. Attempts to define what the adjective craft, and thus craft beer, means have been unsuccessful in the UK, despite the efforts of the players in the industry considered well positioned to do so. Already the purpose of such attempts often is unclear or ambiguous.

Both producers and products can be told apart by the use of the same adjective, and there are many ways to make a distinction. Choosing the facts of the subject for distinction is an arbitrary exercise and will therefore invite criticism, only enabling distinction based on certain facts acknowledged by those coming up with the definition while there might be other facts not acknowledged or unknown to them.

Other factors are even less tangible and thus unlikely to provide the basis for comprehensive definition, but these more subjective factors commonly constitute and are intentionally used as distinctive characters in the marketplace.

Considering the extent and pace of diversification in the industry, a definition is likely to be born outdated. All in all, even meticulous work will result in a definition that is either too vague or too specific, something that is deemed non-comprehensive or arbitrary. The actual associations with the c-word, as well as the specific characters attributed to it, will remain in the eye of the beholder. Hence, in the absence of a universal and concrete definition, the use of the c-word lacks legitimacy, as do the expressions connected to it, such as crafty, faux-craft, etc.

Still, something has certainly been happening in the brewing industry for a while now reflecting evolving consumer demand. These obvious new waves have demonstrated that there is consumer demand for unconventional brews and wider choice (as opposed to explicitly craft beer), as well as new ways and players to respond and seize this opportunity on the marketplace.

WHERE ARE WE NOW?

There has always been demand for the unconventional, exclusive or special. Until not long ago, this demand had been ignored simply for being too small and thus commercially uninteresting. Eventually, though, it grew, and meeting the need for wider choice became easier. Imported products, conventional in their place of origin but not in the UK, fuelled the first wave, as did the revival of real ale, put in the spotlight by the Campaign for Real Ale (CAMRA).

The exploration did not stop there. As more and more consumers realised their latent need for the unconventional, the increasing demand stirred further waves in the brewing industry, calling for new or reinvented local operations to meet this demand. This was further encouraged by the equipment and expertise left redundant by the consolidation of the industry. The cracks in the market gradually widened and deepened, calling for more and more supply and further improving commercial viability.

In recent years, the number of active breweries effectively multiplied in Europe, the increase in the UK being particularly startling. Today, consumers in the UK are spoiled for choice, probably even perplexed by it: according to the *Local Beer Report 2014* published by the Society of Independent Brewers (SIBA), 14–15,000 different cask beers are brewed each year in the UK. Considering that there are also beers available in other forms, theoretically you could try a new beer every day for your entire life. And that is beer produced in the UK alone.

The choice is vigorously expanding through new brands and new types of brews introduced through reinvention, adaptation or revival. This is seemingly a global phenomenon, but the scale and nature might be different from country to country in light of the differences between their cultures of beer drinking.

The unbelievable pace of shift in demand in the UK has set hopes and expectations high, creating the notion of limitless potential. Any unconventional beer sells, and new business failure rates in the brewing industry have been reported as insignificant, especially in comparison to those of new businesses in any other sector. A time has come where the number of people coming out as former or actual home brewers is surprising. You can buy brewing kits in the corner shop or a complete brewery online, and leave a lucrative career behind to start up a brewery by studying the open recipes of model breweries.

This epidemic has brought about a number of concerns, e.g. about product quality and consistency, resulting in less flattering connotations of the c-word which is already attributed to anything unconventional. Consequently, alternative descriptions (e.g. contemporary) started to surface, as well as objections to the (mis)use of the c-word.

There have been other signs of a shifting in the trend: last year saw further acquisitions of new wave breweries by established players in North America, and such activities in the UK for the first time. This outlines the direction of response global corporations are taking to tap into a segment pervading their mature markets.

The increase in demand is no longer met by the production of new breweries alone. Existing players of different ages and sizes are adapting and increasing their production, and exporters to the UK progress with their global conquest by setting up or acquiring outposts in Europe, or the UK specifically. As the landscape of competition is changing and entering the unknown and unconventional, evidence of failures of new businesses in the brewing industry has become easier to find.

The supply chain has grown more complex and diverse than before, and this remains an ongoing trend. While the new wave brews have tunnelled their way into the market through some specialist distributors, bottle shops or pubs, those wanting to trade in them have to have the right skills to keep up with the high pace of change, continuously curating their offerings while managing a widening portfolio.

Future demand remains a big question as consumer behaviour is extremely hard to predict, but awareness of new wave brews and brands is still relatively low in society at large. Through more and more exposure and the education of consumers, the perceptive audience seemingly multiplies year on year. However, as the unconventional becomes more widely available, it risks becoming more mainstream and eventually a commodity – the new conventional. Consumers' experience and preference will inevitably influence the trends, defining some offerings more commercially viable than others and thus triggering consolidation in the marketplace.

The growth of new wave brews has taken place at price levels superior to traditional brews while availability has been limited. The businesses' ability and approach to pricing and availability of these brews can influence change in the effective demand while it is as much determined by the inherent efficiency of these businesses as by government decisions. New wave brews could theoretically replace conventional brews entirely through a sustained better proposition to consumers, but this requires competitive availability and bases for price comparison.

How long will the abundance last? The market share of new wave brews is reportedly still insignificant in the UK, but it is growing and easily absorbs the increasing supplies. However, gaining further market share will become more and more difficult due to the increasing diversity and number of businesses involved. This next phase of new wave brewing will bring fierce competition and risks due to policy making as well as the state of the economy.

The United Kingdom in the EU

The current standing of the European Union (EU) does not seem as strong as it used to be. Its capabilities have been tested by financial crises, both global and at member state level, terrorism and mass immigration. European integration has become secondary to the priorities of the EU member states themselves. Controlling the EU powers and budgets has been instrumental more and more in internal politics, in particular by net contributors.

The UK's approach to the EU has evolved drastically in recent years, and following the general election in May 2015, it became clear that the relationship and dynamics between the UK and the EU needed to be challenged. The prospect of a decisive referendum has been dependent on the success of the prime minister's efforts to implement radical changes. At the time of writing, the PM's efforts have already proved unsuccessful, which implies that he will have to proceed with the decisive referendum. By the time this book is published, it will be more apparent how the UK will relate to the EU in the future.

If the referendum supports an exit from the EU, it will only reinforce the uncertainty that has been present ever since the start of this debate, and this uncertainty will stay throughout the transition. Effecting a change like this will take a few years, which will be spent defining the right status of the UK outside the EU.

The UK is currently part of the EU internal market and customs territory, which makes trading with EU countries more practical and easier, so if the UK exits the EU, it will have to identify a new way of trading with the EU, currently its biggest trading partner. Also, the UK currently trades with countries outside the EU which are covered by EU trade agreements. It is feared that the results of renegotiating trading terms between these countries and the UK will be less favourable than when they were negotiated as part of the more powerful EU trading block.

Changes to the rules of international trade might have major implications on the beer industry as exported beer is likely to be subject to import duty in the EU and thus less price competitive than before. This will affect more than 3,000,000hl beer produced in the UK and sold elsewhere in the EU. As for other implications, potential divergencies between regulations in the UK and EU in the long-term may affect the products in international trade. Beyond the final product, any materials used and sourced from outside the UK might be less available or become more expensive in the UK.

In addition to the trade aspects, outside the EU, the UK would no longer be bound by either the taxation framework mandatory in the EU or the principle of free movement of people. These could potentially have implications for the brewing industry in the UK. The EU taxation system has elements that indirectly influence pricing policies, e.g. maximum VAT level, minimum levels and structure of beer duty or the maximum excise discount for small brewers. The status of non-UK citizens in the beer supply chain, as well as their willingness to work in it, would also become uncertain in the transition.

There is a seemingly realistic opportunity created by the EU exit: the turmoil and uncertainty around international trade and return on foreign investment could affect general supply and cause shortages, as happened in Eastern Europe after the dissolution of their trading block in the early nineties, which the more agile local players could benefit from. As for the size of this opportunity, in 2014, more than

7,000,000hl beer was imported into the UK from the EU: about 18% of total beer consumption.

An exit from the EU would affect the state of national economy at large, though. The impact on consumers, whether in number or purchasing power, will indirectly affect the prospects of the beer industry in the UK.

THE BUSINESS

Brewing beer is practically like producing any other consumer good as it creates a product that is the result of a transformation process. With knowledge (experience and expertise) and equipment, brewers transform primary and secondary materials into a final proposition. Through marketing, it will be made accessible to consumers, and they will enjoy it in ways and under circumstances of their choosing. Many businesses, which spend and earn money, are involved in this relatively simple chain, and the price paid by the consumer is effectively distributed along the chain. If somebody runs out of money, the chain and all businesses in it are disrupted.

Brewing is business: either produce something to make money or become a liability in the chain. Ambition in terms of the amount of money made may be different, but it remains a business. At first, new wave brewing businesses were the result of redundancies brought about by consolidation in the beer industry, people using their expertise and equipment to provide an alternative income to being employed by one of

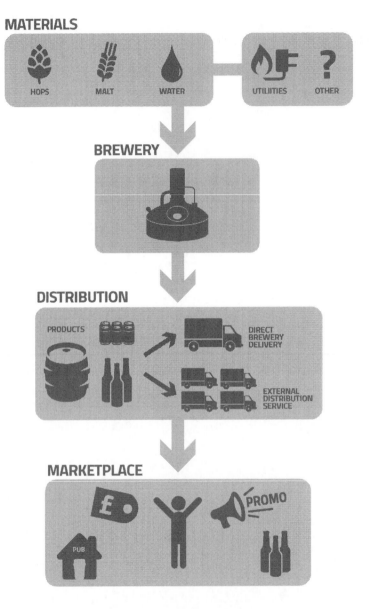

Beer supply chain

the big companies, but some new businesses aim to become alternative global corporations.

Regardless of what intentions you started your business with, there is one common element of business which you cannot afford to ignore: making money. Your other intentions for brewing are not business ones, but essentially they can contribute to your business.

MATERIALS

The primary inputs in brewing are water, malt, hops and yeast. These have their own sorts and can form plenty of combinations. Then there are a myriad of other ingredients used, especially in the brewing of unconventional beers. All in all, the combinations are limitless, and consequently provide an unlimited choice for consumers.

There are secondary inputs essential for the final product, e.g. packaging (bottles and labels, cans, etc.). The process itself and the tweaks therein make some additional materials essential for the operation, e.g. barrels for ageing and utility services.

The selection and sourcing of the materials used for the final product can strategically position a brewery. They can influence the sustainability of and sensitivities to the business model, the consistency and other qualities of the final product, and can provide its distinctive element on the marketplace.

Malt and hops

Malt and hops are agricultural produces, and as such their quantity and quality are weather- and climate-dependent. And, as rightly summarised by the European Commission, in agriculture there is an inevitable time gap between demand signals and supply responses. Small changes in the amounts produced can have big effects on prices as our consumption of food is largely constant compared to other products.

The typical characteristics of new wave brews are claimed to be that they are adjunct-free, meaning they have a higher malt content and thus trigger more demand for malt, and they are rich in flavours or highly bitter, meaning more and wider varieties of hops are required. Considering the pace of growth in new wave brewing, the demand for some of these primary materials will be hard to keep up with.

Europe is a major malt producer, with malt export significantly contributing to the EU trade balance. Nevertheless, this supply, so crucial for brewing both conventional and new wave beers, remains under pressure as demand for beer increases on other continents. Maintaining acreage and total production remains a challenge as farmers explore the possibilities of growing alternative more lucrative crops rather than malt-grade cereal. As a result, malt is sold at ever increasing prices.

Reportedly, adjuncts account for up to 30% of the mash in European beer production, meaning you will need significantly more barley for an all-malt brew. Replacing conventional beers with new wave all-malt brews will have a practical limit: the availability of good quality barley. Furthermore, the growing demand in some regions around the world offsets or even exceeds the decline in mature markets. Malting is also energy-intense, and malt is typically transported over long distances from malt houses to the destination brewery, so energy and fuel prices can easily affect the price.

Of the total surface area used for hop-growing worldwide, 60% is in the European Union, Germany alone accounting for about one third of it. The UK is another of the main EU producers along with the Czech Republic, Poland and Slovenia. The EU has traditionally been a net hop exporter, the main buyers of surplus hops being Russia, the USA and Japan.

However, the availability of both the amount and variety of hops is limited in the UK. Therefore, some of these supplies have to come from faraway places, leaving pricing dependent on the costs of transportation and international trade agreements.

Hops acreage has been fluctuating, so has total production. Statistics from the USA suggest that the hopping rate of beer on average is increasing, as is the number of varieties used in new wave brewing. Some of the most popular varieties are grown almost exclusively in certain areas, which is a major risk in terms of both price and availability.

Consumer preference can shift even over relatively short periods and demand products that are made with more of a specific primary ingredient. Such developments can disrupt the supply chain as all parts of it have to have the right response at the right time. Consumer preference, though, can be influenced by the availability of products, and ideally it can be shaped in such a way to fit the realities of the supply chain and availability of primary materials, both now and in the future.

The number of players in malting is relatively low compared to the number of breweries because of the high capital investment required. Other circumstances as well, like climate or transport infrastructure, can determine the maltsters' profitability.

These factors set certain limits to vertical integration, but collectives of brewers with similar needs can increase negotiation power. Having 'local' sources can limit exposure to the dynamics of the global market and transportation costs, as well as ensuring a smaller carbon footprint. For sustainable final product prices, and thus margins, take into account that primary materials are likely to become more and more expensive. Going forward, diversification of malt and hops suppliers and contracts might lower the risk of lags in the supply to breweries.

Recent shortfalls in certain types of hops have demonstrated the implications of dependence: reportedly, core ranges of some breweries in Europe will be curtailed. However, they have also initiated a more creative and opportunistic way of brewing (including foraging), focusing on and experimenting with relatively cheap materials to get the most out of them.

Water and yeast

The water used for brewing has a definite impact on the quality of the beer. The quality and quantity of the water available will be determinant for the expansion plans of a brewery too. That, combined with the costs of fixing the water quality and content, will define the right place for a brewery and the sustainability of the operation. A consistent water supply is essential for beer quality and taste. If the water quality deteriorates due to environmental impacts, e.g. contamination or pollution, sourcing water through an alternative channel can be significantly more expensive.

Any core ingredient has a major impact on the final product, including yeast, but yeast is probably more exposed to a brewery's cleanliness and capacity to retain the right strains consistently in the brewing and keep them under the right conditions than supply chain issues.

Other ingredients and factors

Without prejudice as to what other ingredients should or could be used in beer, or where they're used in a core product, you have to keep an eye on their price, quality and availability in the long run.

Climate will not only affect crop yields but also influence the energy required for setting and keeping the right conditions, including the temperature of the different brewing processes, and it might be a simple decisive factor for some specific practices, e.g. open fermenting. Looking ahead, some human inflicted changes or patterns in climate and environment, e.g. fracking and water, can affect sourcing materials and should be seriously taken into account.

BREWERY

The brewery is the transformation unit of the inputs into a final product. Schematically, it consists of the premises and the equipment needed. These can be either rented, leased or owned. The brewery will also have non-material assets such as some sort of expertise or experience in brewing and the workforce to perform relevant tasks. The size of the kit and premises, including the areas available for phases besides brewing itself (e.g. storage, warehousing, etc.), as well as the number of people involved defines the capacity of the brewery, as any one of these could cause a bottleneck. (Besides licensed or contract brewing, there can be hybrid set-ups where parts of different brewing operations are combined, e.g. 'guerrilla' or 'nomad' brewing teams or collaborations.)

According to *The Brewers of Europe*, in 2014, there were 6,500 breweries in Europe, and one in four was in the UK, totalling 1,700. This is effectively twice as many as five years before. Their statistics also show that 80% of the breweries in the UK have very little production: below 1,000hl/year.

Institutions, regulators, associations and breweries themselves have categorised breweries in their own rather arbitrary ways. Most such categorisations are based on production or capacity, but the purpose of having categories seems redundant, unless there are actual special treatments or concessions associated with them.

There is one major concession: the Small Brewers' Relief, which grants tax discounts to breweries with annual production below 60,000hl. The EU has a slightly different view and considers 200,000hl/annum small production, and other member states have further interpretations of small. Still, these numbers are combined with additional criteria to benefit breweries from belonging to any category. The primary category used is independence, which is separately and meticulously defined. While this is mainly to avoid the dividing of larger productions into segments with benefits, independence is considered a category for some in itself.

These are objective facts in deciding whether a brewery should have specific treatment or not, and in my view, they are best kept for these purposes. There are, though, so many other ways to put breweries into well-defined categories beyond production or dependence, e.g. composition of ownership or number of owners, management structure, length of time in operation, size of workforce, extent of distribution, etc., not to mention less tangible aspects of a brewery which will not help the application of rules, but will guide customers in the diverse brewery landscape. The ways of distinction will be discussed in the 'Product' section, surprisingly.

There might be another reason to categorise breweries factually, and that is to obtain a particular view of the industry; more specifically, of certain developments over time. Still, the purpose has to be concrete, e.g. to demonstrate the implications of certain policies or regulations on a segment and call for special treatment based on its contribution or role.

Finances

As mentioned before, brewing is business, and as such has a strong financial side. This side can demonstrate whether the business is viable or not. Brewers keep books, file submissions, pay and issue invoices like most other businesses, except you are trading in excisable goods and this means a slightly bigger burden on the operation. In the end, you may judge by the numbers and trends demonstrated in your accounts whether it is worth carrying on or letting it go before further losses are accumulated, despite the fact you might find it hard to quit.

As in any other business, brewers care about the realisation of the best return on their investment, e.g. money, which could be invested in something else, and labour, which could earn a salary doing some other job. Your endeavour might attract others to invest money in your business and expect higher returns than from the financial markets or anybody else's business. You might be looking for rewards from your business other than financial gains, but still your satisfaction will have limits set by the prosperity of your business. Therefore the focus of this section remains unchanged.

Although setting up or expanding a brewery has been proved to be rather easy nowadays, you still have to have money, which you put at risk (as well as that of others involved), and while it can earn you money year on year, that money might well disappear. On the other hand, the business might earn you even more if it is profitable and you decide to sell it. Again, you can find other people to add to your investment, hence lowering the individual risks, but the individual gains diminish as well.

If you would like to maintain your share in your business, and hence in the earnings, you can borrow money and limit the risk by offering some sort of assurance (e.g. material assets that can be sold to pay back the money) or offer to pay the lender an interest rate.

Crowdfunding

There are alternative ways to finance your business that have been used increasingly in recent years. One of these alternatives is crowdfunding which, besides being relatively cheap, has great additional benefits.

The format crowdfunding takes can vary, e.g. in-kind benefits, bonds or equities. Offering in-kind benefits, such as discounts or exclusivity to something offered by the business in exchange for certain levels of contribution, look like quick money at relatively low cost, but in fact, some of the options, e.g. discounts, will even generate more turnover if the investors want to benefit from their contribution. It is doubtful investing in this way in a brewery is a financial decision. The factors in play here are not purely financial, although the investor might get their investment's worth by spending a few thousand pounds on the brewery's products.

Borrowing money is conditional on the interest paid and the risk associated with it. Issuing bonds is a formalised way of borrowing money, and the decision should be based on the same risk and return trade-offs as equity or other investments. However, the assessment of relative risks due to the specific characteristics of the bonds, e.g. risks related to interest or repayment, or liquidation preference in case of business failure, might require expertise in this area. The relative risks, though, seem easier to mitigate through the investors' consumption and promotion of the business.

As for equity crowdfunding, it has received lots of criticism as well as surprising accounts of large sums collected as a return. Reservations about these investments are related to their liquidity and, of course, their yields. Typically, the equities on offer represent a rather slim slice of the business, and although the owners avoid going officially public, it still makes the business seem more publicly accessible. This implies that trading in these shares bought through crowdfunding is rather limited, and unless there is a share buy-back by the business or a potential acquisition of all assets, the likelihood of capitalising on the gains through selling is limited.

Besides liquidity, the actual value of the shares is doubtful too. Analysts regularly criticise or warn about the high valuations of companies in crowdfunding. The valuations are usually based on comparisons to successful sell-outs, multipliers of profit or reoccurring revenue numbers, etc., but this implies that there has to be an intention to sell-out as well as size for it to be worth applying such models. Yet, a business that is not for sale has no price. However, besides the extreme gains, if ever realised, there is an additional benefit for investors. This benefit is associated with tax breaks (SEIS or EIS) for investing in small companies.

There is a growing concern about buying shares in a business related to new wave brews. Returns are more likely to be realised only in the case of a successful exit strategy, and this purely financial orientation of a business can cause conflicts in perceptions about the business (see later in 'Ideologies'). Holders of shares acquired through crowdfunding also have very little opportunity for transactions with industrial investors, simply because the shares they (collectively) own are insufficient to exert any real control over the business. Buy-backs by the business are unlikely to happen, in particular if the valuation has indeed been inflated.

On the plus side, having a crowd is good for easy access to money and to gain a loyal following to promote your brand. Crowdfunding also has the potential to generate larger PR than a loan from a bank would. There is a certain fatigue in crowdfunding, though: an overall impression which is hard to explain.

There are many campaigns and opportunities. You have a choice if you really want to 'invest' in a business in the new wave beer industry: discovery clubs; new or established breweries with unique identities; distributors looking for backing for their expansion. The decision is not solely about the new wave of brewing any more but selecting an exact place for it. In-kind benefits will work for those who are in touch with the business anyway, while bonds and equities will be selected more on the basis of actual returns – most probably cheap shares in ambitious and promising new players than established ones with lower risk but more challenge to their growth.

If anybody is looking for shares and wants to invest, there are plenty of opportunities. They just need to wait for the right one, or the next round of funding of their targeted enterprise.

Collective funding

Collecting investment to establish a business as a community is very similar to in-kind benefit crowdfunding, but there is a significantly lower concentration of shares. Getting involved in such a set-up is only as good as its in-kind benefits, and the only people who will buy your shares will be those who are really into the in-kind benefits offered. Yet in most cases, all they have to do is wait for another round of investment due to the need for expansion. As the shares are rather scattered, they are unlikely to attract industrial investors.

Other funding

Other sources of help with financing your business are only accessible through painstaking applications, but they can still make a difference. There are all sorts of programmes for new and small businesses which might cover your required expertise or contribution through grants or low interest loans, etc. This support can be delivered by local, regional or government institutions and might be available for specific purposes, e.g. export.

Sell-outs

There were two major acquisitions of new wave brewing operations in the UK by international brewers in 2015. The outcome of their stories is not yet written, but these acquisitions shocked the system, both the supply chain and the marketplace.

Amalgamations might start in the guise of some sort of partnership, eventually affecting both the supply and distribution sides of the business as efficiency is improved. The capacity of any businesses that can no longer work with the acquired business can then be used by those who had no access to this capacity earlier.

So far, really small breweries have not traded well on the brewery market. It is the privilege of those that reach a substantial size and manage to maintain pace in scaling up. The financial gain from starting a brewery and selling it might be tempting, and currently there is one sure recipe for achieving this: don't stop scaling up.

Scaling a business has its own challenges, though, and one in particular is cash flow. Another is that there are more and more new businesses with similar ambitions competing for the same space. In the future, there might be new types of acquisitions by the new businesses themselves to maintain the pace of scaling up, e.g. buying successful brands, recipes, exclusive distribution or certain consumer groups, etc. Acquiring space for growth might also imply vertical integrations to improve efficiency, restricted access to certain elements for the competition and limited dependence on other parties.

Management

As demonstrated above, there is far more involved in running a brewery than having brewing skills. It requires business acumen and a diverse skillset to make a profit from the operation. And there will come a time for any (growing) brewery when the founders can no longer attend to both business affairs and brewing beer.

If you feel confident, you might take on managing the business and leave the brewing to somebody else, either a founding partner or hired brewer. The other solution is to hire experienced management, the likely candidates at present coming from a corporate environment and seemingly finding it difficult to think in terms other than improving numbers in one way or another. If this is not the path you think your brewery is on, you will have to be careful in maintaining harmony between the ambitions of the brewery and the management.

Ideologies

There are purposes a new wave brewing business can pursue other than making money. These roles are direct derivatives of an ideology represented in the business and can vary or have a different emphasis for each business. The ideology can be self-proclaimed, or simply perceived and associated with the business by consumers or others in the industry, the perception being a secret ingredient.

Ideology helps convey something unique about how you do business into the final product. The way you do so and its success translate into competitive assets: a special appeal or connection with consumers, or simply a distinctive factor in a market full of a myriad new wave brews that are hard to tell apart. There are many ways products are currently distinguished in the market, e.g. organic brews, brews by social enterprises, brews combining diverse expertise in their making, etc.

The strength of an ideology is dependent on several other factors, e.g. its source, its nature and awareness of it. As for its nature, the ideology can be actual or (unchallenged) deception, and the source is always a person or a group of like-minded people, either insiders or outsiders. The latter attribute ideologies to the businesses based on experience or perception, which might replace or confirm ideologies represented by the insiders. Your leverage over awareness is better if the source of the perception is self-proclaimed, but you can definitely enhance and emphasise certain elements of the perception formulated by outsiders. Without awareness, ideologies will not make any difference.

Conveying an ideology is becoming harder and harder, and general or overused terms, just like the c-word, no longer constitute a distinction. You have to be more precise in describing what you do differently, and how you do it. However, this applies to most businesses that intend to sell more than a commodity, so the noise is deafening consumers and the channels available for education and communication are clogging up.

It remains difficult to predict how ideologies resonate with consumers, and with which group of consumers, but this is what the market can eventually tell you. If you are not limited, geographically or otherwise, you will find the audience to which your ideology is most appealing, or they might find you first.

Vision, mission and values

These terms might seem to be used only in big businesses, but the reality is they are present, if not explicit, in most businesses. They will translate, break-down and put your ideology into context in terms of what your end-game is: why you are in existence, what you want to achieve, how you want to achieve it, etc. The description of your business in this way can make building relationships between consumers or business partners and the producer easier.

Vision, mission and values are represented in your operation and transmitted into your final product. They are incorporated in the price consumers are willing to pay for being able to signal a relationship and derive a status.

This perception cannot be changed quickly, and if you change the course of your business, it might lag or even create a contrast which can affect consumers' general response to your business or the composition of your group of consumers. You have to make sure from the beginning that your perception is aligned to your vision, mission and values – are they compatible and is the match sustainable? It's not enough to pretend to appeal to consumers. In identity movements such as the new wave of brewing, initial followers are motivated by the desire for authenticity.

If you are on a scaling up model, this might be a particular challenge as you grow and look for consumers who differ from your core consumers.

ACCESSING MARKETS

Having a fine product alone does not determine the success of a brewery, and even the best marketing will be redundant if the product is not available to consumers in the way it was intended.

The different markets available for brews are parts of the domestic market or markets abroad. You can sell your product to places in your markets directly or through distribution partner(s). Theoretically there are not any other options. You can, though, apply either or both under certain arrangements by being specific, restrictive or dedicated in terms of the geography or nature of outlets and available markets. The more distributors you have, the more management they require, in particular if their territories are not defined or overlap, but you will no longer depend on a single significant channel.

There are pros and cons to different accesses to markets. Direct distribution will allow you to maintain good trade relationships, and potentially piggyback those to sell a widening product portfolio, as well as having better communication opportunities with your customers, which can provide you with valuable consumer or market insights. However, the cost of sale might be higher, implying concrete limits to distribution in this way.

Wholesalers can offer better, wider coverage and thus access to more consumers, but you share their voice with the many other brands and products they have on offer. It can be increasingly hard to persuade them to sell your products over somebody else's without eating into your margins. A middle man will also cost you money, but potentially relatively less than having your own sales force and systems, unless you have a greater economy of scale there.

Distributors' coverage and potential/target sales volumes need to be aligned to production, thus enabling constant supply. Eventually there needs to be a match between distributors and breweries based on territorial ambitions and scales.

As the landscape of new wave brewing further diversifies, being listed with distributors is becoming increasingly difficult. Distributors are like curators: what they find sellable (a combination of margin and expected volume over a certain period of time) and what they need to sell will definitely be on the top of their lists. They might also favour products that require standard or less care, e.g. in terms of storage, size, circulation, etc. The rule of thumb if you decide to go with a distributor is: the more your product is in demand, the less risky it will be perceived by the distributor.

Distribution should be prepared for promotion and be aligned to anything you do in marketing, in particular what relates to 'place' in that – you might have the best looking pump clips developed, but they're no use if you are only available in bottle shops. Dependent on your aim, you might need to make sure your product is constantly available in strategic places. Partnering with the right distributor can help you jump some of the practical barriers on the market, especially to the places you chose.

There are distributors or distribution systems specialising in new wave brews, but it might still be too big a task to browse their offers as a customer. There is, however, further specialisation on the horizon, geographically, scale wise or in terms of products or premises.

A way of enhancing direct sales is to expand the operation to include distribution for other products: a practical vertical integration in the supply chain. The investment might be shared with other like-minded businesses. Theoretically, distribution networks operated by some brewing businesses could be opened up for 'partnerships' with ambitious and growing new wave businesses, although such precedents in the UK during the 20th century were precursors to some sort of amalgamation.

The relatively high cost of transport and care required in trading in beer can define the limits of distribution within the sustained competitiveness of the product. In the past, this was the major cause of beer being a local product not traded widely or internationally.

The markets

Theoretically, your market is where there is demand for your product. It is the place where you believe there are, or where there actually are, consumers who, knowingly or unknowingly, want your product, and can afford it. The last element of the description of market suggests that there needs to be an equilibrium between demand and supply dependent on price, which will be discussed in detail in the 'Price' section.

Until not long ago, there had been supply of mainly conventional brews to satisfy a broad mass demand. Nevertheless, a latent demand for other beers started to surface and triggered supply of such brews. It happened over several decades, and started with the efforts by CAMRA in the 1970s. These efforts were aimed at retaining the choice existing then as well as ensuring that the quality of beer would not gradually deteriorate, and the campaign to raise awareness of consumer taste and consciousness and their evolution has been successful ever since.

At first, imports from other places offered the sought variety, then some successful experiments, inspired by the successes of similar activities elsewhere, gained traction and served to diversify consumer choice further.

In some European countries diversity in beer has never been an issue, but the concentration in the UK was very dominant. There has always been a demand for products that are different to what is obviously available, but the size of the demand might not be sufficient to risk exploring it further. Experiments and pioneers made consumers realise what they had been missing and thus paved the (high)way for thousands of enterprises to tap into the new wave of brewing.

Local market(s)

The British are considered a beer drinking people. Beer consumption in both absolute terms and per capita is superior to most EU countries. Theoretically, even if you only had a small group of loyal consumers, you could sell a great amount of beer, and chipping off a small piece of the domestic market for yourself might need you to be quite big.

The market in the UK looks fertile for ambitious or determined businesses. The sale of new wave brews has reportedly increased significantly year on year. Nevertheless, describing this market by numbers is a difficult exercise, and scrutinising the numbers is even more difficult. There has been a flood of numbers, and every now and again a number is realistic or good-looking enough to become quoted more than the others. We take that as the correct number, but we no longer have any idea what it actually means and where it came from. Most information about a category already lacks an exact definition, and there is hardly anything specific about nice round numbers.

For example, market shares can be measured in volume or value terms. The former can be production, sales or consumption, while the latter can be gross or net, but the source of information used for measurement (e.g. statistics, reported data, etc.) and the standard level of error in a measurement are just as crucial for interpretation. This list of issues with numbers is far from comprehensive.

While there are sub-categories within the beer market, there are also higher levels of the market. Beer is part of alcoholic beverages, which is considered part of the general beverages category. Within each category there are interdependencies. Although the different types of alcoholic beverages are not considered direct substitutes for each other, overall attitude to alcoholic beverages can make the composition of alcohol consumption shift. In fact, the differences within this category, acknowledged by policy making, as well as any potential government intervention can directly influence shares. By and large, alcoholic beverages are just part of a consumer basket the size of which is a precursor to the trend for all categories therein.

As for absolute market size, any historical data should be cleared of influences to ensure the organic development is depicted. One of the problematic influences is price as changes in average price levels can be instigated by the producers themselves or as a consequence of an excise increase passed on to the consumers. Price elasticity might be different in different price segments. There is also an ethos that in the new wave of brewing consumers tend to put more emphasis on quality instead of quantity. While it is very hard to judge, if it is true the potential market size will be dependent on the conversion rate and not the total beer market. As for shares, percentage points can constitute simple calculation errors or imperfections, in particular considering the small numbers and many sources as well as the pace of market evolution.

I am of the view that there is a credible way to estimate the market size and that is by its net value, i.e. the underlying money available for the businesses involved. This value is the total value minus the taxes (VAT and excise) paid. It might not be the most appealing analysis for policy makers or consumers who might simply feel like purses, but the net value of the market will indicate what is actually available for businesses in the sector.

It sounds simple, but unfortunately it is not. This analysis requires data of all products sold and the actual price they are sold for to the consumer. Considering the number of potential points of purchase, that is rather impossible. Breweries' output can still be measured, though, as can all taxes paid by them. The challenge, although less than that of the previous solution, is that the progressive excise system brings overall production level per producer into the calculation. Otherwise, if the value is gross, the value of the market might grow with each tax increase, but that would not be proportionate to the change in the bottom line of the business.

All in all, the national market in the UK is seemingly open to deeper penetration by the new wave of brews, and there is political support for the producers thereof, although the UK recently introduced a licensing system for wholesalers of alcohol, i.e. anybody who sells alcohol to other businesses, which covers breweries and distributors but excludes retailers. It is called the Alcohol Wholesaler Registration Scheme and it sets no higher requirements than those lawful businesses were expected to meet practically already, but the concerns surrounding the new scheme are over the processing and enforcement of registration. From April 2017 retailers will also have to ascertain they buy alcohol from only registered wholesalers. While it seemingly is not a big issue for businesses, it still increases administration and raises the barrier to starting a business. It is supposed to be a one-off registration, but future changes to premises and company information will have to be notified too.

International markets

Export has been supported in many ways by UK Trade & Investment. The trade balance in beer has a deficit for the UK: there's almost thrice as much beer imported than exported. There are markets where beer consumption has increased rapidly, mainly on other continents, but where market access and price competitiveness of brews from Western Europe are still to be confirmed. There are other more mature markets where UK brews, including the new wave, are already present and gaining further traction, but analysis of their performance in these markets is too scarce to outline a wider scheme for export.

Some brewing businesses have furthered their economies of scale through seeking export opportunities, which in turn have benefited them both locally and internationally. There are brands available globally that sell in a vast number of countries and are transported across oceans without ending up in a non-competitive situation in their destination market. On the other hand, international competition is booming. The new wave of brewing has presented itself in many places, and its proposition to any destination market needs to have something unique; something, besides being an import, that is not available or obvious in products already there. Another challenge of export is the transportation time and cost which indirectly deteriorate price competitiveness as well as lowering remaining shelf life for rotation.

There are some strongly beer export-minded countries, while the UK still has to build its beer-exporter reputation as well as overcoming the old-fashioned image of British beer. Most of the new wave brews are still primarily produced in casks in the UK, which limits the potential or ambition to export. Cask ale is a distinctively British proposition, its short life span as well as the lack of infrastructure to serve it elsewhere making it a rather unattractive product for export.

One particular destination for exports is the EU, the great thing being that it is relatively simple to trade beer to other EU countries. There are no trade tariffs, and managing excise was made easy through EU-wide systems. The internal market has abolished market access barriers, e.g. the imported beer compliance with the purity law in Germany, but the illusion of the EU internal market is a confusing one. While the brew in itself will be accepted in most countries, there might be national requirements to take into consideration, e.g. the presentation or labelling of the product or the local waste management rules and systems.

If your destination country has specific labelling requirements, and in most cases they do require product information in their official language(s), the way you present your product in the UK will not be compliant with the destination market. You have several options. You can implement the requirements and adapt your product presentation to cover multiple countries, which obviously has limits. With the number of countries you intend to export to and specific national requirements, you might need to diversify your product presentation and establish ranges for different groups of export countries. You could leave compliance issues to the importer or distributor, but there might be technical or legal obstacles in doing so, and you will have less control over the look of your product in the marketplace.

A potential nightmare for export is a country with exclusive requirements, i.e. where the presentation must be as required and there is no leeway for either less or more, e.g.

information in one language only. In such a case, country specific presentation is the only solution, which might imply a deterioration in the economy of scale for that market. Within the EU such technical regulations would likely constitute a barrier to trade, but if objections are not automatically raised and if such a situation develops, it will cause disruption until resolved.

There are other ways to be present internationally. You can make your products available in other countries through licensed manufacturing, which could save the transportation and administration costs, but will probably imply reduced margins and less control over the product in exchange for competitiveness in the given market(s). Another more investment intense solution is to enter the international domains further from your home, extending production through sites closer to the destination markets. Some longer established businesses that gained basic awareness through initial alternative export arrangements and activities started launching their own production by setting up outposts, evidenced by new breweries in Europe and the UK.

Competition

It is very unlikely that you are in a position to do everything at your own discretion without any consideration for others or your market. When it comes to competition, the questions you need to ask yourself are: 'Who am I competing with?' and 'What are we competing for?'

Seemingly, the businesses in the new wave of brewing in the UK are fairly collaborative and appreciative of each other's work. There is enough space for increasing the scales of both existing and new players on the market. Furthermore, there is the import of new wave brews, but still the distribution channels and available points of sale are limited in the supply chain and are likely to clog up in the near future.

Recognising or choosing your competition is recognising or choosing your playing field. The general competition of the new wave brews has been conventional, boring beer and the soulless businesses that have blunted consumers' perception of beer by their marketing. Winning over such consumers initially was viable simply by offering choice, above-standard quality, excitement and innovation, which could happen even at a price premium. The general ideology and sympathy for the underdog has made a difference to consumers who gradually opened up and experimented with the new products. The competition was engaged in sorting out their own affairs by following proven patterns. And while their actual response was not obvious, the evolution of the market got their attention.

We are in a phase of competition where markets and shares within it are monitored more vigorously by established players who are responding to the evolution of the market in their own ways, based on the observation of patterns of new wave brews. Spin-off brands tap in, appealing to the new wave brew image and carrying its typical characteristics, and acquisitions of successful brands have started as well and are likely to intensify.

Future activities are more likely to concentrate on the acquisition of talent to leverage on the aforementioned initiatives. The better capacity and power of this talent to portray certain brews or brands will help aim at the consolidation within the extension of consumer choice. The distinction between new wave brews will be less and elements of marketing other than the product will be increasingly used as a competitive means of influencing consumer choice. There will be even more competition coming in the form of import: on a global market, as flagship styles from signature regions become more price competitive and importable, the proliferation of stock keeping units (SKUs) in the UK will be exacerbated.

In parallel, new wave brewers will keep discovering and exploring new niches through which the growth of brews will remain organic, thus converting consumers of conventional beers and opening them up to a new wave of brews. Specialised businesses will form which primarily resonate with their target audience through their identities as well as their ability to respond to evolving consumer preference and gaps on the market. Their economy of scope instead of scale and knowledge of their niche inside out will constitute their primary competitive edge. When all easy-to-find niches are covered, these businesses will start to demonstrate that their coverage is better than anyone else's. They will be able to pinpoint their competitors, and will call them exactly that. Scrutiny of each other's actions will be obvious and shortcomings will immediately be put in the spotlight.

There will come a time when the group of consumers open to new wave brews will not grow as quickly as the supply, and consolidation will become inevitable. Eventually, competing on price to reach better economy of scale will be too tempting to miss, despite ideologies or beliefs. And this mistake will essentially flush the value out of the market for many businesses. Collaborations will have new meaning and will become necessary for survival; gradual integration will begin, resulting in mergers and the potential creation of closer and more formal cooperation of businesses in new wave brewing. At the other end of the scale, there will be a group of smaller specialist businesses who manage to stay out of the scaling competition and consolidation with a particular focus on the market and their respective proposition.

In the meantime, through new technologies and innovative products, home brewing will have its renaissance. Many consumers will return to this more fulfilling non-commercial source of drinking with ease. This way of consumption will grow significantly, but will remain a real challenge to measure or evaluate. Then innovators and specialist businesses will wake a newer wave in brewing and give the pendulum another push towards more diversity in the beer industry, but not necessarily in the product itself.

There is another element to competition that is not marketing or business conduct. This element is policy making and regulation, which will receive more and more emphasis in order to influence market dynamics and the competition. Parallel to the lobby of the industry at large, a more obvious but still underlying layer specific to the competitiveness of a business or group of businesses will exist.

CONSUMERS

In the end, it's the consumers who judge your efforts. You can ensure you are an option on the market by being available and make this proposition more appealing through marketing, but there are other factors playing a role in their choices that you have little influence on.

The individual

The consumer is probably easiest described by factual demographical information which can be useful in marketing segmentation and targeting, e.g. location, place of consumption, disposable income, etc.

Consumers are also individual beings with their own identity which defines how they relate to the world around them, including beer. Without going into deep psychological insights, a consumer's identity will essentially set the baseline for their choice and thus their demand. Their attitude, beliefs and predisposition will play a role in their choices.

The group member

Consumers are members of groups of different sizes and natures. The norms and interactions therein have further influence on their behaviour and choice. Culture or social norms define consumers' attitudes towards alcohol, the type of alcohol and customs or consumption patterns, e.g. place, frequency or amount. You can also refer to peer pressure and opinion leaders within groups of consumers, as both will influence individual choices.

The simplification of choice back in the day would not have happened without consumer indifference. In fact, the styles and brews much criticised now were once selling at premium prices and were welcomed by increasing demand. It was a consumer group, CAMRA, with traditional needs and demands that maintained the (until then) conventional brews in the marketplace and oversaw the quality of the beer choice. And in a way, this started shifting people's perceptions to asking for something different to that which most people chose to drink or know well.

Macro environment

The acceptability of alcohol consumption and the tolerance of alcohol-related harm have been evolving together with the industry. Public health policies and campaigns will shape the environment of alcohol consumption, including types of alcoholic beverage and the amount consumed. Essentially, society is becoming more and more health conscious, and this is used as one explanation for the generally declining alcohol consumption in Western countries.

All in all, consumer choice is a balancing act between the preferences of the consumer as individual and group member under the circumstances of living. The state of the economy and politics influence the values in society, which in turn result in either the individual or the collective being brought forward in decisions.

Nevertheless, choice is always limited in a way as there is curation in every stage of the supply chain based on assumptions about what the customers of the businesses are looking for. If these choices result in what is not acceptable for you, you can look for alternatives or change your system.

Exposure and experience

Consumers could be extremely well disposed towards new wave brews, but it would still be too little if they had no exposure or experience to realise their need and act upon it. They will simply not want or feel like what they have no knowledge of.

Exposure to something new is the first step of eventually realising a need. This exposure to and awareness of a product is usually built through making it available. If the availability is too wide, there is a risk that the product will become less exclusive or lose some of its appeal at the beginning. Wider commercialisation of a new wave brew might also be seen as similar to that of conventional brews, leaving the price tag the only difference between them. The reality of new wave brews, though, is that their availability will be restricted through the practical need to synchronise their scale and their intentions in terms of target market.

If what you feel like is unattainable, it remains a desire; if what you feel like is available to you, it will become your choice. Continuous and consistent availability therefore is the way to connect with consumers and establish an affiliation lasting longer than a fleeting check-in on a beer rating app.

The choice to try new wave brews is a choice to discover and is enabled by exposure. The nature of discovery, dependent on the consumer as described earlier, can range from stepping into the unknown to using some sort of guidance or reference to minimise the risk of disappointment. Further consumption of the new wave brew of choice is dependent on the result of the discovery, which might be regret. Fortunately, in most pubs in the UK you can taste the beers before ordering a pint, but you might skip this in a busy bar and either dive in and try something new or go for something you trust. The option of trial is limited in off-trade retail, and considering that new wave brews are typically more expensive than traditional beers and the purchase requires more effort if you have to go to a specialist shop, the risk perception is much higher.

The level of risk people can tolerate changes all the time, and sometimes, although they are not new to new wave brews, they just go for the one they know, or the new one that is relatively cheap to limit the risk. Sometimes they do so simply because they are perplexed by the choice.

People's experience with new wave brews is what will fuel consolidation, and certain brews will gain more traction than others.

Summary

The new wave in brewing brought choice to the people: choice of unusual styles, tastes and formats over the domination of conventional products. Consumers seem to enjoy and benefit from this choice. This expansion of choice and the limited availability of certain brews have consequences, though: the nature of consumption in the new wave environment changed from finding the one to discovering and identifying the low risk or high reward choices.

The further evolution of the beer industry is highly dependent on how consumers' preferences evolve. Although businesses have little influence over these preferences, they can inform consumer choice through exposure and experience. In that sense, finding a tribe that is specific and well concentrated geographically allows for targeted propositions, better guidance of choice and easier response to any changes in demand.

Consumer research into beer drinking, and in particular that which is relevant to new wave brews, is scarce, and businesses launching into the new wave of brewing cannot conduct proper market research or run focus groups for their beers when their decisions could be greatly supported by such information. The evolution of demand, therefore, is essentially driven by a combination of consumers and marketing by the businesses.

MARKETING

Many definitions of marketing would have something to do with 'inducing change in consumer behaviour'. In simpler terms, it is about if a consumer buys a product it should be your product, and what you do to bring this about is marketing. In this sense, everything that the consumers spend their money on instead of your product is competition. There are products that you obviously cannot compete with, but ultimately you can make your product essential for the consumer and increase the value it represents for them when they decide rationally how to maximise the value of the products they can afford.

The change you will see if your marketing is successful is that more and more people will choose your product over another. As described in previous sections relating to consumers' choice, this journey starts by simply making your proposition available and known. Eventually, consumers will purchase your product for the first time and try it. Provided their experience with it is not dissatisfactory, subsequent purchases may take place.

The ways in which these repeat purchases happen indicate the consumers' level of attachment to the proposition. A repeat purchase may be prompted by the unavailability of a preferred product, with the consumer considering your proposition as a substitute. Your proposition, in this case, is already part of the consumer's repertoire, a space in the consumer's mind shared with other similar products that can substitute for each other or for the absent preferred product. Over time, one product happens to be chosen more over other products in the repertoire – in their absence or despite their simultaneous presence – reinforcing the attachment and thus becoming a regular choice over any other similar products available.

The traditional success of marketing is the loyal consumer who not only purchases a product regularly, but in fact seeks it out when it is not available somewhere. An active loyal consumer converts others, promotes the product, enhances its awareness or perception, etc. All in all, they act as a product ambassador. Marketing is your means to guide a consumer, and all along this journey, it is easier for the consumer to make steps backwards than forwards.

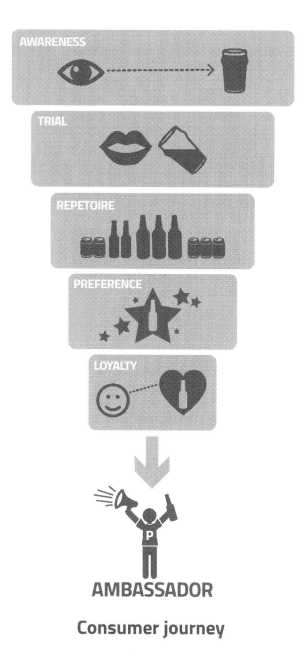

Consumer journey

Marketing of a product is the mix of four elements, typically referred to as the four Ps: place, product, promotion and price. These factors are considered controllable and altered as needed to influence consumer choice best in line with your intentions. Each of these will be discussed separately in later sub-sections.

Marketing of beer has traditionally been bold and universal to raise awareness of a proposition, but it has ultimately been turning the product into a commodity as the propositions were seemingly identical, looking at the factual information alone. Eventually a certain uniqueness was gradually added to the propositions in the form of association between brands and intangible values.

Marketing in the new wave of brewing is slightly different as, first of all, the products are no longer in the commodity category. There are factual characteristics of the products that make a significant distinction, primarily in comparison to conventional brews with mass appeal. Still, this marketing space has become much more sophisticated as products with similar characteristics have appeared within the category. While such redundant marketing is still useful for the overall category of new wave brews, it does not necessarily change the shares of the brands within and can easily be piggybacked by new propositions. The four Ps in the general marketing mix for new wave brews are significantly different to those for conventional ones by long-established businesses, and this is the consequence of the combination of both reality and innovation.

Unless marketing is specifically intended to expand the primary market for new wave brews in general, e.g. collaboration of businesses or as a sector for an entire group of products, marketing will only influence consumer choice towards the proposition of a business if it is precise. Identifying your consumers as well as the market that is accessible to your product can help precisely select the right means for marketing and potentially make it more cost effective. The latter, a factor in competition and competitiveness in marketing, partly lies in being at least as cost-efficient in marketing as the other businesses targeting the same consumers.

Being focused allows you to facilitate almost personal relationships: interactive communications with your consumers to turn them into ambassadors equipped with exclusive knowledge to strike up word-of-mouth campaigns. This close communication will enable you to get to know your niche, your small group of consumers, well, finding out more about demands that you can still satisfy to make your proposition even more relevant for them.

There are plenty of consumers in your niche(s) globally, and hopefully they are within reach. Online marketing solutions have allowed for great levels of customisation, and it has never been so easy to find your audience or for your audience to find you.

The new wave in brewing started with a few consumers who wanted something unconventional. Recent history has proved that inch-wide cracks on the tectonics of brewing can go miles deep and eventually grow miles wide. It might be more difficult to maintain the levels of interaction and intimacy with your audience as the niche expands or your business becomes more diverse.

For some products, like alcoholic beverages, the space for marketing might already be limited due to regulation along the four Ps. This should be taken into account when you select your market and consumers.

PLACE

Unless you sell your product directly to consumers, e.g. in a brewery (online) shop, taproom or brewpub, there will be other businesses involved in its distribution and sales. Ideally, though, you have the notion of control over where your product ends up. And there is more to it than just broad or specific geographies.

You supply a market through the businesses distributing your products, which are actually being sold at and in the ways determined by their places of sale. There might be divergence between places of purchase and consumption, but you can exercise your choice over the places based on who frequents them, how and why they frequent them, and what experience and service these places can provide. Your product can be sold either online or in retail, and the latter category can be either off-trade, e.g. supermarkets and corner shops, or on-trade hospitality venues, e.g. pubs, bars and restaurants. Alternative places or methods of purchase are limited and generally restricted by the requirement of a licence, but their number is growing through delivery subscriptions or vending machines, etc.

There is an overlap between on-trade sale and consumption, but off-trade and online purchases are essentially for consumption somewhere else, mostly in somebody's home. According to the statistics of The Brewers of Europe, half of the beer consumption in the UK in 2014 took place in the home, showing that consumption at home is growing more prevalent. This information does not make distinction between categories of beer or provide explanations, although it might easily be explained by the better price competitiveness in off-trade retail. There must also be an insignificant level of consumption taking place neither on-trade nor at home which might attract further restrictions in terms of places of consumption, already restricted in certain districts or means of transport.

Online beer retailing is gaining popularity with businesses. Setting up an online shop or integrating it into a website has become easy, and there are plenty of businesses to do the actual delivery. However, the turnover generated in an online store is dependent on the number of visitors it attracts. If a website is dedicated to an individual brand or the brands of one specific business, visitors will already have an interest in finding out more about that product or business as they're looking up the relevant websites. This is then a straightforward lead to the online store, but there will be other online stores with multiple brands that can offer the same product with similar information, lower freight cost, discounts or simply the opportunity to mix the products in the basket.

There is growing competition in the space of online beer retail. Running a single-brand or single-business online shop should provide a unique and relevant experience at least as good as ordering from a multi-brand online retailer. The existence of your online store has to be known, and this implies not only promoting your brand and products but also an opportunity to purchase. Single-brand or single-business stores can have a great advantage by offering exclusive products or merchandising as well as customer service representing the unique identity behind the business or products in question.

Traditional retail has limited range in attracting regular customers. This limit is inherent in the physical nature of this type of sale. Consumers show different attitudes and consumption patterns in different places, e.g. throughout Germany, most beer styles have a stronger following in their regions of origin but are much less known, though usually available, elsewhere. The other limit of retail outlets is space: there is a limited number of pumps or taps in a pub and limited space on the shelves.

Space has to be earned, and you can do so by securing an alignment with the ambition of your business and the people you deal with who make the ultimate decisions about holding your product, e.g. owners, managers, buyers, etc. Their baseline intention is similar to that of consumers: maximise the value of the total space available. This translates, in purely financial terms, into a combination of products that are believed to make the most money. If there is space for only one product and there are two similar propositions with similar potential, but product A earns £100 while product B earns £120, they are likely to choose product B. Still, product A could become the preferred choice by applying a formula considering factors such as:

- Margins alternative to a standard rate, e.g. progressive margins

- Actual behaviour and ambitions of the person in charge

- The marketing strategy of the retail outlet and its match with your propositions, e.g. gluten-free, organic or other themes

- Non-financial considerations, e.g. the trouble of changing from an old offer to a new one and depleting old stock, ordering and administering another supplier or having a single supplier for the entire space to cover overall administration, the need of the space available, etc.

- The overall potential of the available space, taking into account cannibalisation, complementary effects of offers or any other interdependencies

✪ The advantages of working with your product or business, e.g. your services and sell-out support, reciprocal marketing, etc.

The relationship you or your personnel can build and maintain with retailers will define your success in credibly elaborating this formula and adding different aspects to it for a well-informed decision.

The obvious consideration when selling in specific places is: if the product is not available, it will not sell. If your keg is in the cellar but not on tap in a pub, if your bottles are in the storage and not on the shelf of a small retailer, you are not going to sell that product. Only your most loyal consumers will actively seek out your product even if it is seemingly unavailable.

Your product strategy can adapt to some of the challenges of gaining space in the right places and switching focus between available product formats to generate exposure in the face of constraints. For example, you can still be present in a pub even if not on tap by being on the bottled beer list. The size of your portfolio and your focus therein can make listing with places either harder or easier, dependent on their formulas.

When you know your preferred places, you will know how your products will be sold. Thus you can influence consumers' experience with your product, its visibility, look and feel as well as customer information and service, etc. Even if you do not own the places or supply them directly, you, your personnel and your product or brand ambassadors have to observe and ensure your standards are maintained. Ongoing cooperation with the places your product is sold in is a source of valuable insights, too. The outlets probably know their clientele; they can induce or observe changes in it and spot and highlight opportunities you will not have spotted, e.g. a shortage in somebody else's supplies.

Navigating the market of new wave brews grows more and more difficult. There is a new business with new products popping up every day, and related news can be overwhelming. In addition, existing breweries will certainly be releasing special, new or seasonal brews every now and again. Selecting the right offer for a retailer can be paralysing: even if you know the favourite categories of your clientele, the match may not always be flawless, and in addition, the supply, even on the core range of businesses, may fluctuate. The need to manage relationships with breweries individually will proliferate, and the complexity will only increase until there's a massive consolidation of the market. Until then, and most probably afterwards too, retailers will need to rely on those on top of sourcing and curating a portfolio for everybody in their distribution network. Not so surprisingly, this represents a barrier to accessing the right places already on the market, and as the general products portfolio expands, the competition for space will become fiercer.

The power in scarcity

Your can approach and select places to create a network of a few strongholds with severe restrictions on others' products being sold there or even exclusivity for you, providing for a sustainable scale of production. You have to be able to maintain access and price for your core of regular consumers at these places in the face of growing demand and higher prices you potentially could charge. At the same time, you have to maintain value and earnings for the places in your original network, even in the case of you gradually opening up to new types of places or areas. Your product may have become a reference point for places or areas as well as being their distinctive factor: part of their marketing strategy, which will make up for them refraining from changing or rotating portfolios and offering more variety.

This is a strategy based on scarcity, loyalty and ambassadors working together with a limited number of places while crucially maintaining constant availability of the reference product(s). The whole experience surrounding the product will be enhanced by its scarcity; the environment in which it is savoured; the adventure for beer-discoverers in seeking these places and finding the product, which is more than anything a beer from their local grocery store would offer for the same price.

Additional barrier to places

There is a long history of bonding between on-trade retail and brewers or other businesses in the beer industry, be it ownership, management, supplies, loans, etc. This often constitutes a barrier for new market entrants as the places where their products could be sold are in a way closed to listing these products. The system in the UK has been looked at and challenged over decades, resulting in a long history of interventions. Paradoxically, a system that has protected small businesses in the past now constitutes a barrier for them through its evolution. While interventions have changed the course of this evolution, they have also had unintended consequences: new issues have emerged and a mature system has been gradually degraded.

The latest such intervention is the Market Rental Option (MRO) for tenanted pubs which is supposed to provide the option for publicans to go 'independent', renting their premises at actual market price. It is still to be seen how publicans will respond to this opportunity, but as their first opt-out comes with the renewal of their contracts, the change to the system is likely to be spread out over years in an effort to avoid potential shocks to the market.

This is an opportunity for businesses in the new wave of brewing which had struggled to get into places. When considering changing to paying market rent, publicans will potentially need to hold more lucrative products, and the new wave brews should deliver and confirm these products. New wave is, however, not for all pubs, and the publicans' deliberation will go beyond only beer.

The current sole suppliers to tenanted pubs ease the selection and sourcing process of the entire offer beyond beer, and the prospect of opening up to thousands of new brands can deter publicans. All in all, though, the MRO is a great means for publicans to choose the more lucrative way of going forward, either by staying tied or going independent. It is also an opportunity for new wave brewing businesses and collaborations of these businesses to replace traditional ties.

Ultimately, there is an inherent symbiosis between retailer and supplier. They both want to sell, and by doing so maximise their profits. For a supplier with an interest in both operations, the sum of profits is what matters in the end. Without an interest in retail, if the profit pool is divided, the supplier is more likely to concentrate on the profit from the supply operations alone, and this might affect the profitability of the retail end.

The need of new wave brewing businesses for places that secure continuous access is growing. While the competition for on-trade places is intensifying and there is much turbulence due to the MRO, the first logical step still seems to be an owned outlet such as a taproom or brewery shop. Owning any other premises constitutes major investments, but having an interest in establishments can help exert influence over what is sold there.

PRODUCT

What do consumers actually buy? Beer is a fermented alcoholic beverage that is made of malt. It is presented to the consumer in different formats and different ways. The packaging and accompanying service in on-trade venues contribute to the sensory experience of beer through look, touch, smell and taste. The act of consumption is also likely to deliver audible signs (opening a bottle or can, clinking the glasses, etc.) or carry an emotional surcharge through the atmosphere inherent in the place of consumption or the conditions under which the beer is consumed. All in all, there are plenty of factors to the experience the physical product delivers. Some of these are specific to beer and distinguish it from other beverages, while other characteristics help the distinction between beer products.

When you choose between products, you choose those that are expected to give you the most satisfaction through the factors mentioned above relative to the sacrifices required. In this sense, sacrifice is more than just price. Any effort that needs to be made to obtain the product, including transport, waiting time, etc., is taken into consideration, either knowingly or unknowingly, rationally or irrationally.

A consumer's choice is highly dependent on their expectations regarding the satisfaction a particular product brings. A brand has to manage these expectations, carrying a section of values which enhances their association with certain product qualities. A brief product description and assumptions about its quality might not be enough to distinguish the product significantly, and the time and space to communicate these in the course of purchase are rather limited.

A brand carries associations beyond product qualities: it carries an identity. The beer industry has favoured identities of product brands over those of producer brands, and has benefitted from this as product brands are sold and bought more easily without significant deterioration of the values painstakingly associated with the product through years of promotion. This multi-brand strategy has evolved and worked in a global environment through mergers, acquisitions and by offering choice between brands, as well as by mitigating the risks involved in exposure of a single brand.

Businesses in the new wave of brewing typically have a different approach. They will have one brand identical or close to the company name for all their products, which makes sense as it is already hard enough to build one brand in an environment with thousands of other businesses trying to build their brand(s) as well. The brand a business uses ideally represents generic and authentic distinction for the entire range of products they offer as well as being fully aligned to their ideologies and values. This helps kick-start new products added to the portfolio through the existing generic awareness of the source and the identity associated with it. It also comes in handy when introducing a product that is on sale for a limited period of time.

There are pros and cons to each branding option. As for the businesses in the new wave of brewing, a single brand for all their product necessities that their 'core range' must be consistent and fully representative of their values. Any other products added to their portfolio will fall within the scope of their brand, and a wrong limited edition can affect the base brand selling their signature range. Crises or flaws of authenticity can undermine the brand, and selling out to another company will be more difficult when the producer's identity brand is practically annulled or significantly adapted.

On the other hand, a single producer brand can easily develop wider appeal and reach 'mainstream' level.

PROMOTION

In this book, promotion means any sort of communication or broadcast aimed at enhancing the association between a brand and its values as well as the identity behind it. The primary channels of promotion are advertising and, to some extent, public relations (PR) through different types of media. Traditional advertising can transmit associations with the product to the masses through channels such as billboards, TV, etc. These are commercially more relevant to businesses whose presence matches the wider reach of the audience of these channels. PR is a rather neglected area for building product brands for reasons explained in the previous section, i.e. branding disconnect between products and the companies behind them.

Businesses in the new wave of brewing capitalise more on PR for their products, benefitting from following the common strategy of using a single brand for both producer and products. PR provides a different level of reach through a diverse range of channels, from local radio stations to international specialist press. However, following the proliferation of brands in the beer industry, the PR noise has become deafening, and businesses need to shout or use the best targeted outlets to make themselves heard by the right audience.

As these businesses do not really try to appeal to the masses, sometime bad PR which is loud can be better than good PR which is not heard by potential consumers. On the other end of the scale, any action inherent in the operation and any internal customer within the supply chain can transform into an opportunity or channel to enhance or diminish the perception of a brand. The supply chain can effectively be mobilised through winning prizes or awards. As long as PR is authentic, or is in line with what consumers think is authentic for a brand, it can only help associations.

Businesses in the new wave of brewing are innovative and creative in promotion. Collaboration has become an abundant practice. The resulting product, a special typically limited edition brew, is made by a combination of the inputs and assets of two or more businesses. The factors of the collaborators, including their nature and character, are usually fairly similar, and the businesses involved are compatible. These collaborations also enable the effective combination of PR and alternative promotional capabilities. The result usually is excessive.

Similar hype can be created by other limited offers, e.g. extremely small batch products with a short shelf life or exclusive 'vintage' findings. Recent examples show that some of these offers can sell out in a matter of days, and this period may become even smaller if it includes advance booking – capitalising on the gap between demand and attainability.

Collaborations can serve many purposes other than promotion. Actual collaboration is the only way to build an identity with a collaborative nature for your brand, which is still a quite unique distinction on the market. It can create an overarching image of a mutual brand, which enables transfers or adoption of values by the brands involved. Collaborations across borders can have strategic businesses purposes. Considering the international expansion of some breweries towards UK soil, this might prove a path to form alliances and establish platforms to resolve potential competitive issues. It can also accelerate export market entry by piggybacking the channels and reputations of the local collaborator(s). Collaboration is also possible between businesses in different phases of the supply chain, e.g. a supermarket chain and a brewer, or a brewer and a distributor, to create something exclusive and benefit all parties involved.

Businesses in the new wave of brewing effectively use new waves of promotion and gather huge followings on social media with targeted campaigns and interactivity. The education of your followers (with the aforementioned PR efforts) initiates further waves of word of mouth promotion, with consumers talking to each other about your brand. This is a particularly effective tool in gathering more followers or guiding them in their consumer journey. One avenue of online interactivity and promotion is crowdfunding, mentioned earlier in the 'Finances' section.

Social media is something that businesses without a legal counsel do well. It is something most people in your business know, use or feel passionate about. A person or a group of people who are social media savvy and enjoy instant interaction can manage the genuine profiles of a brand. In businesses more exposed to scrutiny, though, running a social media feed is similar to any other business operation, i.e. it has to go through formal clearing before anybody presses a button.

Rules for advertising are relatively stringent for substances with regulated or controlled consumption. Social media is supposed to be covered by the UK Code of Non-broadcast Advertising, Sales Promotion and Direct Marketing issued by a self-regulatory body, but the code has neither statutory power nor prohibits any concrete practice explicitly. If the code is breached, The Advertising Standards

Authority, an independent body, will start the investigation based on the complaints received.

Currently, the domain of alcohol advertising and promotion can be seen as ambiguous, and as a controversial matter it will eventually be subject to further restrictions or even statutory regulation. This could pose a major challenge for single-brand businesses in the new wave of brewing: communication of corporate brand is usually less restricted than that of consumer brands, but if there is only one brand used for both producer and their product, it might be difficult to tell their purposes apart.

PRICE

Price is a powerful element in the marketing mix. Setting the price will not only define how much profit you can make on the product, but also the level of demand and supply on the larger scheme of economics. There is a price point where demand equals supply. If the price is too low or too high, there must be a shortfall or surplus in supply.

Price is a distinctive but not inherent feature of the product. Currently, the price of new wave brews is significantly higher than that of conventional brews subject to mass appeal. From this point of view, the price can be indicative of product qualities, e.g. it's more difficult to make or more expensive materials need to be used, or the level of supply. The latter can indicate that the relatively high cost per unit is due to the lack of economy of scale, but based on the theory of balance between supply and demand, low supply can command higher prices through the notion of exclusivity or limited attainability.

The price of the product has to cover raw materials, the running and margins of your business and other businesses in the supply chain, and taxes. Setting your price, you choose your playing field and competition. Seemingly, though, competition among new wave brews is not based on price alone, and competing with the prices of conventional brews produced at a global economy of scale is out of the question. Based on 2004 data from the USA, the average cost of beer production declined substantially until annual production reached 1.2m US barrels, which is about 1,400,000hl, an amount seemingly far out of sight for most businesses in the new wave of brewing. Consequently, prices of new wave brews are likely to remain significantly higher than those of mass-produced beer for a long time.

New wave brews have entered the premium price category and created a price category above that. Competition based on price within the premium price range is not apparent. The slight differences are partly due to the varied alcohol levels of the product and hence the excise paid. The other explanation is related to the principle of premium products: premium pricing necessitates that prices remain stable. If the price is reduced or the product is otherwise discounted, perceptions of its qualities, reinforced by the premium price, will diminish. It is very difficult to raise the value, and thus price, of a product once its price has been dropped. Dropping the price of new wave brews without substantial gain in the economy of scale of production to compensate for this will only decrease the value, and thus the money available for the businesses involved.

For businesses in the new wave of brewing, there is more emphasis on competitive advantage of scope than on scale, i.e. on their ability to produce small batches of a wide range of products instead of a limited range on a large, more cost-efficient scale. This might also influence the way businesses go about pricing. They might find alternative solutions, like auctioning instead of offering a product at a fixed price to benefit from the surplus demand.

One of the most significant elements in price remains tax, accounting for about 30% of the off-trade retail price. Of the price, 16.7% is VAT and approximately 10–15% is excise dependent on strength, production level and, of course, actual retail price. Essentially, the government has the highest margin on the product. Change in the rates of VAT and excise will directly affect cash flow as well as the bottom line of the businesses in brewing.

Changes in tax levels, though, can present an opportunity to reset or adjust margins or fine tune price. The price changes due to tax increases can incorporate more than the absolute tax increase: producers can decide how much of the increase should be passed on to consumers or absorbed by the producer. The price increase can also be higher to round up to more comprehensible and comparable numbers.

Excise

In the EU, applying excise on beer is a must, and there is a minimum level required. The EU, however, does allow member states to introduce reduced rates of excise for small independent breweries, provided it is not less than half of the standard rate.

In the UK, the progressive beer duty was introduced in 2002, and this is considered to have been the ignition of new wave brewing in the UK. It was implemented ten years after it had become an option through the adoption of the directive of the EU excise framework for alcohol in 1992. The production limit to benefit from the UK excise concession is significantly lower than the 200,000hl/annum limit in the directive, and the UK limit also seems low compared to other EU member states. However, as opposed to the practices of these member states, the UK maintains a gradual increase of excise rate and not a tiered system.

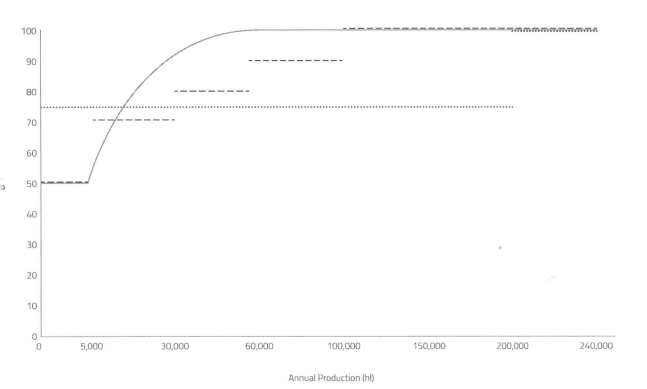

Illustration of tax discounts in three EU countries by comparison of actual excise vs. standard rates

This concession and its limits have been criticised, in particular for the arbitrary nature of its cut-off limits. The theoretical difference between the lowest level of excise provided for small brewers at maximum 5,000hl/annum production and those for mass-produced beer of more than 60,000hl/annum production is approximately 5p/%/pint. This difference significantly diminishes with the production level, e.g. at an annual 30,000hl production it is only 1p/%/pint. (Calculations are based on excise rates as of 1 January 2016.)

In the UK, the approach to connecting the excise rate so closely to actual production incentivises brewers of less than 5,000hl annual production to remain small, but on the plus side, above this level the excise increase is gradual and less likely to hinder scaling than a tiered system.

The introduction of the progressive beer duty system is believed to have made small brewers more competitive vis-à-vis those players on the market who enjoy economies of greater scale, and most small brewers would find this crucial for their business. It is interesting to note, though, that the take-off of new wave brews is not strictly dated back to the introduction of this system. And Italy, where a similar new wave of brewing has taken place, does not have the system for small brewery excise concessions in place at all.

In addition to those who criticise the arbitrary limits and do not benefit from the scheme, even those who do benefit express concerns related to the system in the UK, as is summarised in the *Local Beer Report 2013* by SIBA:

> *In spite of their overwhelming support for Small Breweries' Relief, even a majority of the brewers who completed the survey … agree with the suggestion that duty relief has encouraged the growth of too many breweries. Competition is increasingly fierce.*

The excise system as it is in the UK is an instrument to collect government revenues and a means to support smaller brewing businesses. Excise on alcoholic beverages in general is:

- An indirect tool to regulate market sizes and can affect single categories

- Often used as an influencer of international trading in these products, e.g. by making one mainly imported category less price competitive

- An influencer of cross border trade. Differences in excise rates, and thus prices, between neighbouring countries instigate smuggling

- Not solely a financial instrument. Excise is much emphasised in public health, in particular in relation to affordability and thus overall consumption.

Excise in the EU

The aforementioned EU directive 'on the harmonization of the structures of excise duties on alcohol and alcoholic beverages' was formally adopted in 1992 and is still the reference framework of excise duties for all alcoholic beverages, including beer.

Despite its age of more than two decades, the directive is still considered apt, except for some technical issues that have come about over the years. Among these issues are the different classifications of identical products by different member states, the lack of harmonisation of excise rates creating big differences in prices among EU countries, and that the duties are being used as trading barriers.

These technical issues were investigated in a study which was requested by the European Commission and published in 2010. The policy options the report identifies include the resetting of the minimum excise duty rates, i.e. the introduction of one for wine, and the revalorisation of existing minimum rates by up to 44% (the increase of price index between 1992 and 2010). It outlines the possibility of maximising duty rates at EU level to eliminate huge price disparities. As for the classification issues with beer, it suggests the introduction of a maximum alcohol content level, e.g. 12% ABV, for better distinction between what is beer and what is other fermented beverage – an excise category separately defined. The report also addresses the lack of harmonisation, including the use of exemptions for small producers which is said to 'account for a small proportion of the market' but is able to 'create significant distortions for mid-size producers' as well.

The European Commission started evaluating what actually needs to be done to the original directive in 2014. As part of this work, in 2015, an EU-wide consultation was launched on a number of relevant issues, and the member state tax administrations, industry stakeholders, including beer producers, and the general public were invited to share their views. The issues in the consultation document indicate what the European Commission believes needs addressing or can address. Those relevant to beer mention classification of beverages, common rules governing the application of reduced rates for small producers across the EU, including a review of the limit (200,000hl) and its market distortion effects, the extension of reduced rates to other products and permission for production of categories other than beer for private consumption.

Although the aim of the consultation is to collect more information and evidence, this preparatory phase will be processed in the justification and baseline for any further legislative action by the European Commission. The consultation ended in November 2015, but as of March 2016 the contributions had still not been published. It remains to be seen, therefore, to what extent the particular views of the 6,500 breweries in Europe were expressed or represented.

Although EU legislation is a tedious process, and market implementation can take a few additional years, the EU-wide rules on excise essentially define the space and direction for further evolution of the alcohol beverage industry in Europe, including beer in the UK. Most of the interventions considered will have direct or indirect implications on the new wave of brewing. The harmonisation of the rule for reduced rates across the EU might imply, for example, a higher small producer limit in the UK or implementation of a tiered system as opposed to a gradual increase system, which will have major consequences for many operations, including potentially increasing competition from other EU countries. If similar reduced rates are applied to distillers, another wave in the alcohol beverage industry could onset and represent more competition to new wave brews. Capping excise duties, although unlikely to be further considered by the European Commission, will most probably affect the rates in the UK, which levies one of the highest excise rates on beer in Europe. And there are many more hypothetical scenarios.

Trading in an excisable good carries inherent challenges for businesses. There is a relatively high level of administration and control involved to ensure the receipt of government revenues. Private import or home production of excisable goods is regulated for a reason as these can easily gain a commercial nature and constitute tax-evasion. The UK is in a favourable situation without neighbours on land who could make cheap alcohol in-flow much easier, which is a practical factor enabling the UK to have one of the highest levels of excise, and thus alcohol prices, in the EU. Still, illicit alcohol has already caused problems for the UK and triggered measures such as the recent Wholesaler Registration Scheme.

Other means of price regulation

Although excise and VAT theoretically command a minimum price of a product, health policy might like to see higher prices at the bottom end of the market without the intention to collect more revenue (except for the VAT on the price increase). There have been such calls in the UK, with Scotland even having passed legislation in this regard, but following a challenge by the alcohol industry, the European Court of Justice ruled Scotland's statutory minimum price unlawful. In the light of this ruling, proceeding with such measures will be rather difficult.

Theoretically, the minimum unit price in Scotland would only have affected the very bottom of the alcohol beverage market. The price increase would have squeezed the gaps between price categories, which might have been looked at by the involved businesses as an opportunity to persuade consumers to trade up to higher price categories. However, cheap alcohol would have remained cheap and available in other parts of the UK and could have instigated (secondary) trading in these products. It would also have created a precedent in Europe and a system that could further escalate minimum unit price any time. Considering that excise duty rates are set in Westminster, if Scotland is determined to curb problem-drinking, other available instruments, such as restrictions of consumption in space or time, will need to be considered which could have even worse implications for the entire supply chain in the alcoholic beverage industry, including reduced sales or higher operating costs.

Any statutory cost element that can no longer be entirely absorbed by the businesses will influence the price. These elements can take the form of any new tax on goods or services involved in the beer supply chain, e.g. environmental fees for packaging.

Summary

Excise will remain the primary instrument for (minimum) price regulation of alcoholic beverages, and thus of beer. The introduction of alternative taxes or elements of excise (e.g. a high strength beer tax, which is already in place) is likely to be more intensely debated. One of the reasons might be the exponential growth in the number of excise payers, in particular in brewing, which puts massive burden on tax administration and might require the simplification of the tax system, e.g. through changes to the Small Brewers' Relief .

The potential changes to the EU excise framework can intensify the new wave of brewing in Europe outside the UK and thus increase competition. Furthermore, they can affect the Small Brewers' Relief and relative pricing of alcoholic beverages in other categories. Any potential EU legislative action on excise of alcoholic beverages will be subject to immense lobbying, and will shift the competition from the marketplace to Brussels.

INNOVATION

Innovation has been considered one of the main drivers in the new wave of brewing. In fact, innovation has been continuously changing the landscape of beer. Innovation does not have to be restricted to the product alone. The advancement of science and technology has changed, and will keep on changing, how we grow crops, source materials necessary to beer, actually make beer and at what scale, how the whole distribution works, and how and where the consumer can access the product.

Regulators have a crucial role in this: they will need to be vigilant as well as innovative themselves. They will need to watch the marketplace and respond with appropriate regulation to 'legalise' the use of certain achievements and enable their commercialisation. They will also have to be innovative in regulation of the industry in line with other policies as well as providing space and incentives for further development.

We might see innovation in marketing, e.g. pricing policies or digital and mobile engagement increasingly used for promotion. The next few years will see further evolution of hospitality venues and alternative places where beer is sold to counter the temptation and ease of consumption at home due to enhanced online opportunities, decreasing delivery costs and new home brewing appliances.

WHERE NEXT?

Reportedly we live in the time of the craft beer revolution. In my view, the revolution has already happened; it's over now, just as we don't call the maturing and decline of mass-produced conventional beer a revolution any more. The revolution took place with the realisation of the demand for something unconventional on the market and the commercial response to this.

The term craft beer no longer has a definitive meaning and only confuses beer drinkers. Nevertheless, we live in a time when anyone can seek out and access any beer they feel like, acting upon previously latent needs and even realising new ones simply by being exposed to new products brought to life by creative businesses. It is the pendulum swinging backwards from commodity to distinctive products, indicating a new cycle (a wave) of evolution in the beer industry. Whether it's a trend or a fad is no longer a valid question; the question is what players with a variety of distinctive characters in the industry actually want and what these players will do to achieve that.

Their decisions, determination and conduct will define how and which brews are to penetrate society further, which businesses will be able to be in charge of looking to the demand and how long this cycle will last.

Different players have different interests: status quo, overhaul or restoration can all be legitimate business interests, while indirect stakeholders, e.g. governments, consumers, etc., also have an influence. Ideally everybody wins, but this is unlikely to be subject to some higher grand plan; rather it is likely to be through instincts and a good deal of game theory.

This new wave of brewing has already proven there is way more to beer than what was on the shelves of supermarkets or offered in average pubs until recently. It has brought a great variety of beer styles and compositions, and it's easy to see that the proliferation of brands and products is causing clogs and fatigue in the supply chain. Hence simply releasing more new or unique beers will not be enough to sustain the new wave. Now, it requires more than just having great ambition, drive and imagination to succeed as a business. The marketplace evolves at a great pace, and success is becoming more dependent on the brewers' capacity to keep up and adapt.

Parallel to the exponential growth in demand, the number of businesses interested in looking to supply this seemingly lucrative demand is increasing. The new infrastructure further inflates the existing global capacity, and the need for utilisation of any surplus will trigger decisions that will change the marketplace, although it is hoped that most of the surplus capacity owned by businesses with global reach will be channelled into the waking Asian markets.

The collaborative attitude among brewers might suffer in the face of demand expanding more slowly than the potential supply by the growing number of businesses in the new wave of brewing. There has to be a change in trends, and competition will be interpreted in new ways by the businesses which are either new or choose not to scale to succeed, while the bigger businesses are likely to get even bigger and/or their product will be scaled with help from other businesses and thus compete on efficiency from many perspectives. The smaller players will need to concentrate on their strength, whatever this may be.

We will soon see a slowing down of the increase in the number of breweries, either by less start-ups or higher failure rates. There will be a better allocation of self-assigned roles among newer breweries and more emphasis on diversification.

NEW WAYS OF THE BREWING BUSINESSES

From a holistic perspective, the world of business is changing, and beer is part of the change. This new world provides fertile ground for a new wave of small businesses that do what their predecessors, their bigger versions, have done, but in new ways, giving something more to consumers than what they have been given before. And consumers like to have more: consumers like to have your heart, soul and sweat (not literarily) with your product. Their purchase is their expression of appreciation, proving they like or even love you, what you do and how you do it. Hired executives and managers changing from one well-paid position to another are rarely loved, even by their own employees. The only source of affection in their direction might be that of investors looking for better return on their money.

Besides being the pursuit of your passion, starting a business to surf the new wave of brewing can be a good alternative to what you have done or could do elsewhere, provided this combination of making a living, having fun and achieving something gives you more satisfaction.

In this equation you will also find the place for potential. When you pay your own wages you have no safety nets, but you have no limits either. The potential of extreme returns is sometimes the baseline of an enterprise where growth is the driving force and world domination is the mission. If you manage to grow at an incredible pace, you will soon become your own boss, but will be left with nothing that really reminds you of why you were in the business in the first place, i.e. brewing beer.

How you perform and evolve in new and growing roles can define your exit from the endeavour. The two major acquisitions of new brewing operations in the UK in 2015 demonstrated that it is feasible for a small business to scale in good financial health and have prospects.

Currently, premium prices are paid for new wave brews, and consumers derive status from the symbolic values transmitted by the product. As discussed in the 'Marketing' section, the product in the new wave of brewing carries a close link between its values and those of its producer. The purchase of the product is an expression of a consumer's relationship with the producer and identification with their values. The new wave of brewing is essentially a matter of enriched and compatible identities, and the way the identity of the producer evolves can have a huge impact on the consumers' perception of the values transmitted by the product, and hence on their willingness to pay (premium) for it.

However, there is hope for those intending to scale: research shows that as identity movements mature, consumers focus less on the identity of the producer. Eventually the focus will shift from the producer's identity or the production process itself to how specialist-generated products serve the consumers' need to exercise choice. Hypothetically, the more mainstream new wave brews get, the less important role the producers' identity plays. Significantly altering the organisations' identity and deviating from the identity of the producer as construed by the consumers will then seem feasible.

Despite the theoretical feasibility, extreme potential does not have to be the primary force of an enterprise. There seem to be categorically alternative ways of leading businesses in the new wave of brewing. Their level of potential and sustainability then is a matter of matching the type of business and the way it is managed.

Think globally and act

The world's largest beer conglomerate was one local brewery only three decades ago. Through strategic mergers and a spree of acquisitions it now has more than 1,000 brands. It has also been active in showing and gaining an interest in the new wave of brewing.

The number of businesses in the new wave of brewing that aim at global domination is visibly growing, both in the UK and elsewhere. Some of them are likely to be scooped up in money-heavy acquisitions, providing they successfully realise their potential. Recent examples and future acquisitions will further fuel the competition for scaling to reach a level worthy of such considerations. Those businesses that are just about to set off on this journey will feel left behind, and so will their potential investors.

If being acquired is not an attractive idea for your business, the relative competitiveness of your scale will deteriorate over time unless you yourself acquire other businesses. There are ways alternative to formal acquisitions to ensure you out-perform a consolidating market in scaling, e.g. specific partnerships, contract brewing, mergers, etc., but such actions will undermine your absolute authority over the future of your business. With the scale of production, competition grows incredibly, especially compared to operating locally. The nature of competition might involve hurdles erected in your business's path intentionally, and a heterogeneous ownership can more easily decide, in the face of these threats, to accept an appropriate offer. Also, as you grow, the impact of individuals will diminish, and in such a measured risk-averse environment, it will become more difficult to implement breakthrough ideas. The focus will instead shift to diversification, forward planning and risk-mitigation.

The 2013 survey of SIBA members shows 'a clear and impressive indication of local brewers' commitment to growth'. This might be taken as their expression of priorities, but it is unlikely they will become the next large beer conglomerates in the world. More than half of the breweries that responded to the survey in 2014/15 have less than 1,000hl annual production, and about 85% have less then 5,000hl. There is also a hypothetical limit for almost 2,000 breweries to grow in the UK. The current annual beer consumption of 44,000,000hl is 22,000hl/year/brewery, while international trade can influence this number both upwards and downwards.

Businesses that currently benefit from the largest economises of scale will be in a difficult position: a battle on two fronts. On the one hand, there have been massive mergers and acquisitions, and there might be more to come in the pursuit of even better economies of scale to increase competitiveness through consolidation and leveraging synergies. On the other hand, the businesses' mature markets are becoming swamped by a vast number of new brewing operations converting more and more consumers. Their response to the latter is due in light of the growth of the segment of new wave brews, but protecting their market shares implies diversification contrasting with their ambition to improve economies of scale. This balancing act can be difficult to incorporate or exercise internally in traditional business cultures.

The means available for established businesses to tap into the market of new wave brews are acquiring established brands or launching a spin-off brand that claims similar qualities to the new wave brews. When these businesses possess a brand that is competitive in the segment of new wave brews, they will be in a position to influence the direction of consolidation within the segment due to their capacity for promotion and distribution.

There is also the paradigm of opportunism alien to many businesses with greater economies of scale. Businesses in the new wave of brewing have either capitalised upon a newly identified demand or their capability, superior to others, to look to a demand without a strategy on how to build steadily and maintain the market share of the product in question. Seizing an opportunity can constitute a tactical move which can generate sales and allow for changing course eventually, including delisting of the product.

The constant opportunity presented by the new wave of brewing lies in a general curiosity about the new, which is demonstrated by the proliferation of both businesses and products on the new wave market. From this point of view, one business can seize opportunities in many forms, e.g. under the guise of a new brand of a product similar to its established ones or those of a new but not independent brewery. It is still to be seen how these practices will be scrutinised and where their limits are.

One other thing you need to consider if you are on the path to world domination with a brew is your consistent material supplies. Scale of brewing demands scale and consistency in agricultural produce. This might be difficult in a potentially extremely fast paced expansion trend going through years of constant changes in climate.

As their conquest progresses, businesses are more likely to concentrate on areas most relevant to them and leave the less fertile territories behind. This will enable them to focus on the consistent long-term supply of products through production and sufficient sourcing of their ingredients, etc. The wilderness of specific demands in niches and local markets will only spoil their potential economy of scale.

Think and act locally

The size of mature beer markets is unlikely to grow, unlike the number of businesses within them, and this implies that the average size of businesses will become smaller and smaller. Unless there is massive consolidation, the gap between small and average businesses, and thus between their competitiveness, will diminish.

The businesses that are on a scaling track will compete with those on the same track, and to keep improving their economy of scale these businesses will need to get rid of the parts that hold them back. These will be the corners of the marketplace where incremental gains are relatively high-risk or high-cost compared to the core market of the business. Therefore, while certain businesses will grow, others will specialise, entering and occupying these corners of the marketplace.

Considering the limits of distribution set by cask conditioning, cask still being the most popular and feasible format among smaller businesses in new wave brewing, being local is reality, unless they set out with a deliberate decision to scale. In fact, there are examples of businesses that decided to skip the local phase entirely, but meeting demand that is not concentrated geographically requires wider distribution and dealing with the complexity of international trade. All in all, the future for businesses that do not intend to scale lies in specialising locally.

Being local not only affects small businesses but also the surrounding communities. The people in these communities will have special habits, preferences, values, etc.; they will share something local. Identifying and appealing to their local identities can hardly be done any way other than being local too.

Based on average per capita consumption, a brewery with the capacity of 5,000hl/annum can theoretically cater for up to 8,000 people. If a brewery of this size has a 1% share of the market, it has the potential to cater to a total market of 800,000 people depending on the reach of its distribution system. However, the distribution capacity of small businesses is rather limited – over 80% of beer is sold within 40 miles of the brewery, according to the *British Beer Report 2015* by SIBA, which translates into a well defined area. Price manageable at this scale will not gain a greater share of the market. A reasonable 10% share of a market within a population of 80,000 people will enable leveraging efficiencies in distribution. The ambition of local breweries to improve their competitiveness should therefore be concentration as opposed to increasing scale, and by doing so they will create space for other like-minded businesses.

Being truly local has a significant distinctive power over the local market. It enables businesses to restrict availability to local networks, allowing for natural scarcity. Local breweries improve diversity in their area, can boost tourism and shape customs. Businesses in the new wave of brewing are the best placed to add a point of difference most relevant to their community to their portfolio, capitalising on their reputation and contributing to their environment, and the contribution is reciprocal between them and their community. The small businesses utilise local resources and help local people earn their livelihoods while creating something they can enjoy.

Competition for a local brewery can only come from another local brewery. Those businesses that build on heritage, becoming embedded into local society and customs as well as knowing their customers best, will not have external competition. Their boundaries are defined by their capacity beyond what is required to keep their local stronghold.

Another element of local breweries' competitiveness is their economy of scope as opposed to economy of scale: they are more agile in responding to supply chain issues and changes in consumer demand. Being able to produce a wide portfolio, swiftly switch from the production of one product to another or launch a new one can support the business's core range as well as mitigate any risk therein.

Beer might become a more emphasised part of tourism if interest in local brews continues to grow. There is space for international beer attractions similar to Germany's Oktoberfest. Hopefully certain areas within the UK will claim a prestigious status in the categories of beer or beer-experience and become ultimate destinations for beer enthusiasts.

There seems to be a growing commitment by smaller breweries to being local. There are slight differences in the results of the 2013 and the 2014 SIBA members' survey in terms of priorities in investment. Most importantly, 'Brewing Capacity' has dropped in ranking while 'Pub Acquisition' has risen most in importance over the year. The results also show that the highest priority is still 'New Equipment', which together with the rise in importance of 'Systems Upgrade' indicates that independent brewers' investment is targeted at efficiency to maintain focus on quality, local environment and sustainability issues such as the better use of resources and supplies (e.g. energy, water, local ingredients, etc.)

Local businesses contribute to local communities in many ways: paying local taxes, employing people, attracting visitors, etc. In so doing they support many other local businesses and thus help retain life in more remote areas.

Business diversification

Creating or integrating something different into the business can mitigate the risks of dependence on core commercial activities. This diversification can follow a pattern outlined in the marketing strategy or simply be used to contribute to the bottom line of the overall business. The industry has already provided many practical examples of how to diversify your business.

Having or enhancing hospitality in relation to the brewery is a great channel for sales, and it grants control over the consumers' direct experience with the brewery. The addition of taprooms, brewpubs and other hospitality establishments, e.g. hotels, will further diversify the places of consumption and consumer experience. These establishments will not only generate sales from own brews, but from services provided or products on sale too. Venues like these can provide space for many events other than consumption alone and further contribute to tourism. They can also enable cooperation and reciprocal support with other such establishments.

The distribution of own goods can be combined with other products to improve cost efficiency of visits as well as creating interdependency between products. Specialisation or partnerships in this distribution model are other viable ways to diversify. The product range can also be diversified with other alcohol matching the profile through distilling or beer-hybrid drinks, e.g. beer cocktails, custom made batches to order, etc.

Essentially, looking to any part of the supply chain, e.g. hops or grain for malting, can give a boost to the perception and reputation of the business. However, diversification of the business might be less favourable for those aiming at selling-out as potential buyers will probably focus on single commercial activities and will not tend to value the parts less relevant to them.

The challenge of alcohol

In the long-term, one of the major challenges for the new wave of brewing, and the beer industry in general, is the regulation of alcohol beverages. Alcohol is a substance with addictive properties and its consumption can be harmful. Although there is no definition of what exactly constitutes harmful use of alcohol, almost 6% of all deaths in 2012 could have been attributed to it, according to the World Health Organisation (WHO). It is not only believed to be a causal factor in plenty of diseases, but it can also result in harm to people other than the consumer. All in all, alcohol poses a significant economic, health and social burden on society.

The WHO members endorsed a global strategy aimed at reducing the harmful use of alcohol and thus the related burdens on society. Their strategy outlined policies and other potential interventions for implementation, based on which the European Union formulated more relevant and specific strategies to reduce harmful alcohol consumption. While setting health policies remains at the discretion of each country, the UK agreed to adopt these strategies, which will certainly influence the direction and content of new measures.

There is very little businesses can do to avoid or limit the pace of further regulation. Taking responsibility over how their products are consumed is probably the best they can do, but there are significant practical limits to this. Some businesses in the alcohol industry have been subject to allegations that such campaigns are indirect promotion, allowing one producer to prevail over another through values gaining wider traction within society. Other businesses are not in a position to take responsibility over how their products are consumed or simply refrain from doing so, which implies that the collective effort of the industry is not universal enough to rely on. Additionally, despite the best efforts of businesses, the outcome cannot be guaranteed. Any one incident of consumers 'disobeying' rules or common sense regarding harmful consumption can instigate a response to limit the risk of similar incidents further.

Alcoholic beverages remain controversial products, and as such are subject to policies and interventions similar to those implemented or being tested on other controversial products. Most of the target areas recommended by the WHO directly affect the businesses in the industry of alcoholic beverages. These areas translate into elements of the marketing mix and essentially reduce consumption through policies that limit exposure to alcoholic beverages, making them less available, appealing, consumable or affordable to consumers, and the range of inventive measures is growing.

Exposure to and availability of alcoholic beverages can easily be restricted by reinforced regulation of advertising or by affecting the number of places where consumers can find or purchase them, e.g. a more stringent licensing regime. The space of remaining retail outlets and the products displayed within them can be restricted by reducing the total 'facing' area of the displays or offering a choice based only on a standard price list. The accessibility of the outlet will remain dependent on authorised opening hours or other special conditions beyond age-control, e.g. authorising consumers to purchase alcohol following a risk assessment.

Home brewing might fall victim to these availability limiting efforts too, either through outright prohibition or the regulation of access to the supplies required, as it is seen as an additional health concern due to quality issues, relative affordability and the potential to permeate the commercial channels. These limits will be justified by the risks outweighing the benefits, as those with an interest in brewing or transition into the industry can do so relatively risk-free by honing and gathering their knowledge or expertise in the almost 2,000 commercial business.

Consumption can be limited through its dimensions, i.e. its space and time. While places of on-trade consumption are already limited, consumption in other places, mainly in public areas or in the home, can also be contained by adding conditions such as no drinking when youths are present or without the company of somebody abstinent. The idea of restricting the time and/or volume of consumption is concerning, and it is likely to be affected indirectly through limitations on purchases, e.g. sales permitted only during certain time periods or guidelines for allowance, in particular in off-trade retail, both in terms of volume and regularity.

The most creative area of regulation is the appeal of the product. Theoretically, appeal is a group of factors, e.g. types, flavours or CO_2 content, distinguishing between the product most in demand and the other products on the market. Restricting appeal eliminates these factors and thus limits choice. Alcohol content can be limited within each category, or the appearance of the product can be undermined by lots of compulsory information that compromises the brand and product story, e.g. more health messages, guidelines, warnings or forbidding the use of certain expressions. The regulations might even go as far as standardisation, prescribing the exact content and format of labels or the presentation of a product, e.g. minimum volume, can or bottle, etc.

Even if alcohol were not already expensive enough in the UK, consumption could easily be influenced by price level based on the simple fact that demand has negative price elasticity: if the price increases, demand decreases. And there are many taxes that can be charged and increased to affect the price. These combined with a relatively high minimum serving size or product volume can easily deter consumers.

Some of these measures might sound extreme or far-fetched, but let us not forget, alcohol was prohibited for several years less than one century ago in the USA. Although the policy was deemed wrong and was eventually overturned, the obvious way to reduce the burden of harmful alcohol consumption is to reduce alcohol consumption.

Interventions usually have consequences other than their main objective, sometimes unintended, and these consequences will play an increasingly important role in relation to alcohol policies. The actual change in the marketplace is dependent on a combination of pace, magnitude and a sequence of measures as well as their implementation and enforcement. The primary risk associated with regulation is the creating or facilitation of a secondary market of a grey or black nature that allows low product standards and loss in government revenue.

Let us hope that the new wave of brewing will not need to deal with any of the extreme restrictions mentioned in this section and can shape and influence more favourable policies for businesses. Their challenge is to create a solid distinction between beer and other categories of alcoholic beverages to support different and proportionate treatment in policies. Demonstrable differences in (harmful) consumption patterns between conventional brews and new wave brews can enhance the position of the latter for the future.

The role of industry bodies

In light of the long-term challenges and issues faced by most businesses in the new wave of brewing, representation of their interests will be crucial in the debates to come. Considering that most of these businesses will not have the resources to deal with policy and regulation, their representation needs to be coordinated. This is best done among businesses of similar nature and character so their collective position can be more specific. Otherwise a position that is acceptable for the whole of a wide and diverse group of businesses, a common denominator, will be too generic.

Credibility of representation is as essential as the position itself. It might be tempting to talk on behalf of consumers or other businesses in the supply chain due to their indirect links, but that can undermine the standing on issues specific to the member businesses. Representation should solely focus on the collective interests of the members, although it can undertake to align and inform positions of other stakeholders within the supply chain as well as to mobilise their representations. Still, credibility stems from legitimacy, so an industry platform should not provide ground for discussions of a dubious nature, and its workings should be formalised and transparent.

Considering the proliferation and increasing diversity of businesses as well as innovative set-ups, industry bodies can often be challenged regarding their mandate and representativeness. Businesses in the new wave of brewing can be categorised in many ways, and a representative has to be specific regarding the definition of their members and membership. Ideally, all businesses would be represented by a body, and the representations would cover all specific groups of businesses without significant overlap. There is, though, an 'economy of scale' for industry bodies too, and they compete for members by addressing selected issues that divide or attract businesses in the given sector.

Theoretically, total representation could be ensured by a general requirement for every business to choose and join an industry body based on the specific interest they represent. This could take the form of a modern system of guilds without creating monopolies or erecting barriers to entering a market. The system of enrolling new businesses should be as automatic, easy and burden-free as possible.

To ensure the sustainability and competitiveness of a group of businesses, it is important to have a vision for the membership and a clear map of the horizon showing any obstacles. The communication thereof to the members will not only help identification within the group of businesses, but also set direction for all members. In addition it might facilitate commercial undertakings by the group of members that they would not realise otherwise, e.g. coordinated purchasing groups, distribution networks or generating primary markets for members through mass advertising of the common characteristics of their products and education of the public.

There are elements to sustainability that are not specific to the new wave of brewing but are related to businesses in general. Education, information and support relevant to planning and running businesses will help improve statistics on the performance of the membership. Some business decisions will require information the individual members would not be able to obtain alone. Industry bodies are usually better positioned to gather insights and collect information for these decisions as well as building evidence for cases in policy making. Information might already be available from other organisations or more easily obtainable via cooperation, so maintaining a network of relevant organisations can be useful.

Industry bodies can save and enhance the reputation of their membership by the facilitation of alternative settlements in disputes and the promotion of fair competition among members while raising awareness of unfair competitive behaviour from the perspective of the membership as a whole. The industry body should proactively seek to level the playing field as well as addressing issues in relation to regulation and policy making negative or disadvantageous for the membership at both national and EU level. A neutral outcome is good, a positive outcome is better.

National regulation of the product, miscellaneous technical requirements and trade agreements are sources of constant threat to market access. If the membership is interested in exports, these threats should be monitored and responded to, potentially coordinating cross-industries or borders.

IN THE CRYSTAL BALL

It's 2020 and craft beer, as most frequently reported, has a 4% market share in the UK, although this number still varies significantly within the range of 3–7% depending on the definition the market research companies receive from the relevant commissioning industry body or government agency. The primary measure of share is still volume, in which the total beer market has declined, but its net value has been constant. One thing is obvious to everybody, though: there are more beer brands and products generally available, although the products on offer have become rather hard to navigate given the coexistence of conventional brews in unconventional presentation, unconventional brews in conventional presentation, unconventional brews in genuine presentation and import brews that are not obvious imports.

Retail chains have the most popular styles listed, although with a limited selection: typically each has one signature or mainstream brand, most of them distributed by businesses that only had conventional brews in their portfolios a few years before. The focus has not really shifted from the average beer drinker who still consumes 96% of the total beer volume, but retailers offer craft brands with continuous supply and more flexible prices compared to the rest.

Many other less exposed brands are available from specialist off-trade retail outlets, the number of which has risen significantly over the previous few years. However, these retailers now realise more turnover and better margins from their online divisions, and partly because of this, consolidation is on its way to create regional hubs and networks with innovative delivery solutions to stay ahead of competition. Subscription discovery clubs are run by most retailers, but these are losing traction due to the multitude of relatively cheap events and other channels frequently used to introduce new products. The creation of an international online beer retailer delivering to consumers all over Europe and sourcing globally is being discussed widely, in particular in the context of public health issues associated with distance selling.

The decline in the number of pubs has slowed down and is close to stagnation as a result of businesses in the new wave of brewing focusing on this channel. Many businesses have invested in a hospitality venue as a secure place of sale or seized the opportunity presented by the Market Rent Option. Pubs that do not have craft beer on offer seem to have become less competitive, and industry recommendations include offering both draught and bottled craft beer, or at least installing a craft beer vending machine. These machines have started to spread, recent adjustments to the system making them even more likeable to publicans.

The previous few years have seen more and more businesses in the new wave of brewing successfully scale up. They have executed their strategies superbly through investments in other businesses or brands to become businesses with real international influence, enhancing their presence abroad through either owned or licensed manufacturing.

There is a common notion, though, that the link between brands, businesses and locations has weakened, and this is eventually underlined in a study commissioned by an industry association. Discussions are taking place with CAMRA about a potential campaign for all beer, as opposed to just real ale, that is actually produced by British businesses on British soil.

Local brews by local businesses have become lucrative. Cask conditioned beer is in the prime of its renaissance and is used as a major competitive and distinctive factor for these businesses. Local brews are only distributed in the proximity of their origin, making these beers exclusive to hospitality venues close to the brewery. Also the production of these breweries in formats other than cask is absorbed within their area or at events organised by local businesses from more than one area as they travel around.

Beer is contributing more and more to local tourism: besides offering special beer, the experience is further enhanced by the cooperation of local businesses, e.g. by offering brewery trails, festivals or supporting other attractions. These alliances also tend to unify the channels of sourcing raw materials and distribution. Some areas have become so dependent on the cooperation between the local businesses that it has resulted in allegations of limiting competition and blocking local market access, but these concerns are regularly dismissed by competent authorities.

Core ranges are becoming less important for many local brewers as a consequence of them benefiting from more freedom in deciding whom and what to supply. These businesses are prolific in producing seasonal brews and special editions. The word craft, and its associations, is gradually being replaced by another c-word: creativity. Agility, resource efficiency and ceaseless imaginative product development clearly distinguish successful businesses from those that have a more static portfolio. The resulting brews remain sold at a significant price premium, and this premium association with the brand is frequently leveraged to promote products other than beer, including farm produce, other alcoholic and non-alcoholic beverages, cosmetics and services.

Following another recent shortfall in certain sorts of hops, contracts have transformed into speculative businesses. Hops producers and primary merchants are introducing know-your-customer policies to ensure the quality and reputation of the hops are not affected by their eventual appearance on the secondary market, but there are allegations that long-term contracts are more intensely used as a competitive instrument, thus limiting access to some primary materials.

The review of the rules of alcohol advertising to transform the current system into a more explicit statutory regulation has caused turmoil among businesses in the new wave of brewing. The community is divided based on the awareness of their brands: those who benefit from higher awareness are accused of considering this an opportunity to get rid of the more competitive brands who do not benefit from the same level of awareness. After all, the latest report about the new rules indicates that the implications for beer were blown out of proportion and will only bring an insignificant change to current practices.

A concrete proposal is drafted for the abolition of the Small Brewers' Relief, which results in major demonstrations and a massive response from the affected businesses in the UK and sympathetic businesses abroad. This, in combination with the fact that the European Commission's review of the EU excise framework is still ongoing, eventually puts the process on hold. In the meantime, though, the initiative is linked to one of the new wave brewers that not long before was still taking advantage of the scheme. In their response, they admit that they believe this is the only way to sustain and leverage what their generation of businesses had achieved, which attracts support from a number of businesses in the new wave of brewing.

There have been some other changes in trends and practices in new wave brewing. One business with a track record of successful crowdfunding campaigns fails to gather support for their canned ready-to-drink beer cocktails, but they are still launched on the market a few months later. Blogs seem more and more concerned about the deterioration of beer quality and gradual change of recipes, especially of those brews produced by businesses that successfully scaled up and entered the international marketplace. As a result, one of the next industry conferences has an 'Adjuncts' Use in the Most Popular Craft Beers' presentation on its agenda.

DISCLAIMER

The views in this book are those of the author and should not be interpreted as advice. The author rejects any responsibility over how and for what purpose the information presented in this book is used. The author does not have any commercial interests or support that would constitute a conflict with the writing of this book.

FURTHER READING

I enjoyed reading the literature and using the sources on the list below. They helped me identify the most relevant topics for this book and informed my thinking about them.

Books

- ✸ Chris White, Jamil Zainasheff: *Yeast: The Practical Guide to Beer Fermentation*, 2010, Brewers Publications

- ✸ Daniel Priestley: *Entrepreneur Revolution: How to develop your entrepreneurial mindset and start a business that works*, 2013, Capstone

- ✸ Evan Rail: *The Meanings of Craft Beer (Kindle Single)*, 2016

- ✸ James Watt: *Business for Punks*, 2015, Portfolio Penguin

- ✸ Jessica Boak, Ray Bailey: *Brew Britannia: The Strange Rebirth of British Beer*, 2014, Aurum Press Ltd; The Good, The Bad & The Murky, 2015

❊ Johan F.M. Swinnen: *The Economics of Beer*, 2011, OUP

❊ John Mallett: *Malt: A Practical Guide from Field to Brewhouse*, 2014, Brewers Publications

❊ John Palmer, Colin Kaminski: *Water: A Comprehensive Guide for Brewers*, 2013, Brewers Publications

❊ John Spicer, Chris Thurman, John Walters, Simon Ward: *Government Intervention in the Brewing Industry*, 2012, Palgrave Macmillan

❊ József Faragó: *Kézműves sör kalauz*, 2015, Alinea Kiadó

❊ Mark Colburn: *Craft Beer Marketing & Distribution – Brace for SKUmeggeddon*, 2015, Shinerunner Publishing

❊ Oliver Wesseloh, Julia Wesseloh: *Bier Leben: Die neue Braukultur*, 2015, Rowohlt E-Book

❊ Philip Van Munching: *Beer Blast*, 1997, Times Books

❋ Stan Hieronymus: *For The Love of Hops: The Practical Guide to Aroma, Bitterness and the Culture of Hops*, 2012, Brewers Publications

❋ Steve Hindy: *The Craft Beer Revolution: How a Band of Microbrewers Is Transforming the World's Favorite Drink*, 2014, St. Martin's Press.

Other publications

❋ Alcohol Concern: Stick to the Facts: Alcohol advertising regulation that balances commercial and public interest, 2013

❋ British Beer & Pub Association: Beer Story: Facts on Tap, 2015

❋ Court of Justice of the European Union: The Scottish legislation introducing a minimum price per unit of alcohol is contrary to EU law if less restrictive tax measures can be introduced, 2015

❋ Department for Business, Innovation and Skills: Pubs Code and Pubs Code Adjudicator: Delivering 'No Worse Off', 2015

❋ Department of Health: How to keep health risks from drinking alcohol to a low level: public consultation on proposed new guidelines, 2016

- Esa Österberg: Pricing of Alcohol, WHO, 2013

- European Commission: Assessment of the added value of the EU strategy to support Member States in reducing alcohol-related harm, 2012; Report … on the rates of excise duty applied on alcohol and alcoholic beverages, 2004; Evaluation of Directive 92/83/EEC on excise duties on alcohol and alcoholic beverages, 2015; Consultation Paper: Review of existing legislation on the structures of excise duties on alcohol and alcoholic beverages, 2015; Excise Duty Tables, 2016; Study analysing possible changes in the minimum rates and structures of excise duties on alcoholic beverages, 2010; The EU explained: Agriculture, 2014

- Ferment: Experiments in the Global Craft Alcohol Movement, 2015 and 2016

- HM Revenue & Customs: Alcohol Duties, https://www.gov.uk/topic/business-tax/alcohol-duties; Alcohol Wholesaler Registration Scheme (AWRS), 2015

- Jeff Menashe: State of the Craft Beer Industry 2013, Demeter Group

- Jeff Widdows: Risk Management in the Hop Industry – 2016, Wells Fargo Insurance Services, USA

- Jon Øyvind Bjørnstad, Christian Adeler Normann: Beer Industry, 2011

- Macpherson, Erin: An examination of the competitiveness of the methods by which beer has been distributed in the UK focusing on the beer tie agreement, University of Glasgow, 2015

- Matteo Fastigi, Roberto Esposti, Francesco Orazi, Elena Viganò: The irresistible rise of the craft brewing sector in Italy: can we explain it? (draft version), 2015

- Mr. Stout: Your Friendly Craft Beer Sommelier, 2016

- Pete Brown: The Cask Report 2015, 2015

- Peter Swann: The Fall and Rise of the Local Brew, Nottingham University Business School, 2010

- Jo-Ellen Pozner, Michaela DeSoucey, Katarina Sikavica: Bottle Revolution: Constructing Consumer and Producer Identities in the Craft Beer Industry, Institute for Research on Labor and Employment, UC Berkeley, 2015

- Society of Independent Brewers: Local Beer Report, 2013; Beer Report, 2014; British Beer, 2015; Delivering the Future of British Beer, 2015

- The BCAP Code: The UK Code of Broadcast Advertising, v1.2.7

- The Brewers Journal, 2015 and 2016

- The Brewers of Europe: The Contribution Made by Beer to the European Economy, 2013; Beer Statistics 2015 Edition, 2015

- The CAP Code: The UK Code of Non-broadcast Advertising, Sales Promotion and Direct Marketing, v12.2.9

- What's Brewing, BC's Craft Beer Community Magazine, 2015 and 2016

Online sources

- Beer Business Daily (https://beernet.com)

- Beer Today (http://beertoday.co.uk)

- Beeronomics (http://beeronomics.blogspot.co.uk)

- ✼ Boak & Bailey's Beer Blog (http://boakandbailey.com)

- ✼ Brew Geekery (http://www.brewgeekery.com)

- ✼ Brewers' Association (https://www.brewersassociation.org)

- ✼ Business Insider (http://businessinsider.com)

- ✼ Craft Beer World (http://craftbeerworld.co.uk)

- ✼ Crowdcube (https://www.crowdcube.com)

- ✼ Financial Times (http://www.ft.com)

- ✼ Hops & Vines Blog (http://www.hopsandvineshomebrew.co.uk/news)

- ✼ International Hop Growers' Convention (http://www.hmelj-giz.si/ihgc)

- ✼ Original Gravity (http://www.originalgravitymag.com)

- ✼ Stonch's Beer Blog (http://www.stonch.co.uk)

- ✼ the drinks business (http://www.thedrinksbusiness.com)

- The Truth About Equity Crowdfunding
  (http://fantasyequitycrowdfunding.blogspot.co.uk)

- Total Ales (http://www.totalales.co.uk)

ACKNOWLEDGEMENTS

This book is the result of support and inspiration from the people I have had the luck to become acquainted with. Specifically, I would like to thank Laszlo Labody, my sponsor and intellectual role model; Peter Haraszti for his continuous encouragement; Sophie Donoghue for her patience and ceaseless support; Rethink Press for turning this work into an actual book; my former bosses, colleagues and peers; and all my family and friends.

THE AUTHOR

Csaba Babak was born in Hungary. He studied Industrial Engineering and Management with particular focus on Environmental Management in Budapest, then worked in both not-for-profit organisations and private businesses of different sizes. He lived in Brussels, Belgium and Zurich, Switzerland, before moving to London, United Kingdom.

Csaba worked in the tobacco industry for almost a decade and held national, regional and global management roles, primarily in policy making. Later on, he took a short detour into the e-cigarette industry in a senior management role. He had also co-founded an indoor advertising company that helped businesses reach out to young adults in campuses.

Csaba is a keen observer of events on the consumer goods market. He is interested in economic trends and patterns, in particular the sustainability of different business models, and has developed a particular interest in alcoholic beverages due to their similarity to tobacco in terms of policy making. Fascinated by the course and pace of developments in the mature beer markets, he is also passionate about the rise of small businesses, which is why he decided to launch his own business. Beer Me Bags is an innovative merchandising solution for bottled beer retail to increase sale and improve consumer experience at the same time.

Csaba spends his spare time at the ice rink playing ice hockey, listening to all sorts of contemporary music and hanging out with others, discovering the landscape of beer.

Printed in Great Britain
by Amazon